WHAT ARE THEY SAYING ABOUT
THE GOSPEL OF THOMAS?

What Are They Saying About
the Gospel of Thomas?

CHRISTOPHER W. SKINNER

Paulist Press
New York/Mahwah, NJ

The Scripture quotations contained herein are from the author's own translation and the New Revised Standard Version: Catholic Edition Copyright © 1989 and 1993, by the Division of Christian Education of the National Council of the Churches of Christ in the United States of America. Used by permission. All rights reserved.

Cover design by Jim Brisson
Book design by Lynn Else

Library of Congress Cataloging-in-Publication Data

Skinner, Christopher W.
    What are they saying about the Gospel of Thomas? / Christopher W. Skinner.
        p. cm.
    Includes bibliographical references (p.   ) and index.
    ISBN 978-0-8091-4761-8 (alk. paper) — ISBN 978-1-61643-136-5 1. Gospel of Thomas (Coptic Gospel)—Criticism, interpretation, etc. I. Title.
    BS2860.T52S55 2011
    229'.8—dc23   2011042937

Published by Paulist Press
997 Macarthur Boulevard
Mahwah, New Jersey 07430

www.paulistpress.com

Printed and bound in the
United States of America

CONTENTS

For Mike Gorman....teacher, scholar, and friend.

ACKNOWLEDGEMENTS

Though my name alone adorns the cover of this book, there are other important names that deserve mention. So many different people contribute to a work such as this, and many do so without ever realizing their impact. For my part, I remain ever aware of the extraordinary people I am privileged to call family, friends, and colleagues, and I am extremely thankful for those who surround me day after day.

First, I want to express my gratitude to the late Father Lawrence Boadt for both his interest in this project and his enthusiastic acceptance of it as a part of the *What Are They Saying About?* series. I would also like to thank my editor, Enrique Aguilar, for his careful and thorough work on my manuscript. His editorial eye spotted a number of errors, and his suggestions for improvement have made this book more readable and user-friendly.

I am indebted to Dr. Janet Timbie of The Catholic University of America, whose courses in elementary Coptic in 2004–2005 sparked my initial interest in studying the *Gospel of Thomas*. I would like to thank Kelly Iverson and Josh Jipp, each of whom read earlier versions of the manuscript. Their comments, both written and oral, have improved this book considerably, though the blame for any deficiencies should be placed at my feet. I have also discussed portions of my research with Nick Perrin, Simon

Gathercole, and Mike Grondin, all of whom provided insights that enlightened me and directed me to new areas of investigation. I would also like to express thanks to my current dean, Dr. David Hines, and one of my students, Josh Barfield, for reading an earlier version of the manuscript and offering "nonspecialist" viewpoints and critiques. My primary goal has been to write a book that students and nonspecialists can use with benefit. I am particularly thankful that David and Josh have taken the time out of their busy schedules to let me know where I have (and have not) been successful in that endeavor.

I am a newcomer to my current institution, Mount Olive College, and during my short time at the college I have experienced nothing but warmth and collegiality. In particular my colleagues in the Religion Department, Tyanna Yonkers, Neal Cox, Carla Williamson, Hollis Phelps, and Rich Boyd, have welcomed me into the fold and helped smooth my transition to life in eastern North Carolina. I would also like to extend my thanks to Susan Ryberg, the reference and extended services librarian at the college's Moye Library. As I was completing this manuscript, Susan dutifully tracked down a number of hard-to-find resources several times at the last minute and once over the holidays.

As always, I owe the greatest debt of gratitude to my parents, Robert and Linda Boyette. Without their tireless effort, constant support, and stellar example of hard work, I do not know where I would be or what I would have chosen to do with my life. As I raise my own children I am constantly aware of the sacrifices they made and the challenges they faced in shaping a stubborn, hardheaded, and occasionally oblivious son into a responsible adult. Their model of faith and determination has inspired my every move and has opened numerous doors in my life. Every success I experience belongs to them as well. Thanks, Mom and Dad.

This book, which I had hoped to have in print a year sooner, was significantly delayed by two state-to-state moves in two years. A good portion of the book was written during the 2009–2010 academic year in which my family shared a home in Virginia

Beach with my in-laws, Rusty and Connie Carlock. They deserve my sincere thanks for enduring a hectic year filled with uncertainty, anxiety, and quite a bit of overcrowding. Their sacrifices have made possible our future successes. For that I am very appreciative.

By far, the most abundant blessings in my life have come from my wife, Tara, and our three children, Christopher, Abby, and Drew. These four gifts from God make every day worth living and continue to put my writing projects and other vocational goals into proper perspective. All of my labors are ultimately directed toward the end of improving their lives and returning to them a small measure of the fulfillment and joy they have brought into my life. I cannot thank them enough for their dedication, understanding, and love.

Lastly, I want to thank my friend and former dean, Dr. Michael J. Gorman. The first half of this book was written during a very difficult year in the life of my family. During that period no individual showed more concern, offered more support, or sought to create more avenues of benefit to me—and Mike did all of this on his own initiative. Since 2005, Mike has been a mentor to me both professionally and personally. His advice on a wide range of issues has enriched me as a teacher, as a scholar, and as a person. Mike is an excellent teacher and a gifted scholar. However, despite his scholarly acumen and teaching ability, I have been most impressed and impacted by Mike's loyalty as a friend. The Johannine Jesus tells his closest followers, "By this all men will know you are my disciples if you love one another" (John 13:35). In all my dealings with Mike he has truly embodied the spirit of this verse. It is with admiration and tremendous gratitude that I dedicate this book to him.

LIST OF ABBREVIATIONS

ABRL	Anchor Bible Reference Library
AcBib	Academia Biblica
ANRW	Hildegard Temporini and Wolfgang Haase (eds.), *Aufstieg und Niedergang der romischen Welt: Geschicthe und Kultur Roms im Spiegel der neueren Forschung* (Berlin: Walter de Gruyter, 1972–)
Ap. John	*Apocalypse of John*
BA	*Biblical Archaeologist*
BAR	*Biblical Archaeology Review*
BETL	Bibliotheca ephemeridum theologicarum lovaniensium
BibInt	*Biblical Interpretation*
Book Thom.	*Book of Thomas the Contender*
BThZ	*Berliner theologische Zeitschrift*
BZ	Biblische Zeitschrift
BZNW	Beihefte zur Zeitschrift für die neutestamentliche Wissenschaft
CBQ	*Catholic Biblical Quarterly*
CBR	*Currents in Biblical Research*
CE	Common Era
ETL	*Ephemerides Theologicae Lovanienses*
EvT	*Evangelische Theologie*
Exeg. Soul	*Exegesis of the Soul*

ExpTim	*Expository Times*
FFF	*Foundations and Facets Forum*
Gos. Phil.	*Gospel of Philip*
HR	*History of Religion*
HTR	*Harvard Theological Review*
Hyp. Arch.	*Hypostasis of the Archons*
JA	*Journal Asiatique*
JBL	*Journal of Biblical Literature*
JECS	*Journal of Early Christian Studies*
JETS	*Journal of the Evangelical Theological Society*
JSNTSup	Journal for the Study of the New Testament Supplement Series
JTS	*Journal of Theological Studies*
LNTS	Library of New Testament Studies
LTQ	*Lexington Theological Quarterly*
MSJ	*Master's Seminary Journal*
Mus	*Museon*
NedTT	*Nederlands theologisch tijdschrift*
Neot	*Neotestamentica*
NHC II	Nag Hammadi Codex II
NHMS	Nag Hammadi and Manichean Studies
NovT	*Novum Testamentum*
NovTSup	Novum Testamentum Supplements
NTAbh	Neutestamentliche Abhandlungen
NTS	*New Testament Studies*
Orig. World	*On the Origin of the World*
P. Oxy.	Oxyrhynchus Papryi
Presb	*Presbyterion*
PRSt	*Perspectives in Religious Studies*
PTMS	Princeton Theological Monograph Series
RSR	*Religious Studies Review*
SAC	Studies in Antiquity and Christianity
SBLDS	Society of Biblical Literature Dissertation Series
SBLSP	*Society of Biblical Literature Seminar Papers*
SecCent	*Second Century*

SemeiaSt	Semeia Studies
TLZ	*Theologische Literaturzeitung*
VC	*Vigiliae Christianae*
VCSup	Supplements to Vigiliae Christianae
WUNT	Wissenschaftliche Untersuchungen zum Neuen Testament

1
THE *GOSPEL OF THOMAS* IN HISTORICAL PERSPECTIVE

As I sit down at my computer to write I can hear the television news reporting the political events of the day. There are a number of important political issues in the United States right now, and the stakes have never been higher. In presidential press conferences, senatorial debates, and daily sound bites a major discussion in contemporary political discourse centers on the pivotal issue of health care. Some politicians favor the current state of privatized health care while others want radical changes to the traditional model. Still others want slight modifications to the present health-care system while avoiding extreme changes. In short, everyone involved agrees on the importance of providing quality health care for the American citizen, but there is little agreement among the experts on how to approach this task.

This state of affairs mirrors the current situation with the academic study of the *Gospel of Thomas*. Virtually every scholar in the field agrees on *Thomas*'s importance for assessing the picture of Christianity within the first two centuries CE, but there is little agreement on how to approach this enigmatic text. Some scholars want to question every "assured result" of previous *Thomas* scholarship while others feel that the traditional views of *Thomas* are still sufficient. Agreement among scholars remains elusive and, as with the current political landscape in the United States, the stakes in these discussions are high. What we conclude about the *Gospel of Thomas* has significant implications for our understanding of the historical Jesus, the canonical sayings traditions, and the earliest trajectories of the Christian faith. When we attempt to answer questions about *Thomas*'s antiquity, theological outlook, and relationship to the canonical Gospels, we are ultimately deliberating on traditional understandings of early Christianity versus contemporary theories of alternative Christianities. A leading *Thomas* scholar, Stevan Davies, states it this way:

> Thomas' independence or dependence [on the synoptic Gospels] determines whether it will be considered of importance in reconstructing the actual teachings of Jesus, or relegated to being simply a piece of modestly interesting evidence about what a group of second-century Christians understood the canonical Gospels to be saying....If the Gospel of Thomas is a list of sayings which are taken from the canonical gospels, either directly (through literary rewriting) or indirectly (through secondary orality), [then] for information about Jesus we should turn to Thomas' sources: Matthew and Mark and Luke. But if Thomas is a list of sayings written down independently of the other gospels, then Thomas is as valid and valuable a source for the teaching of Jesus as they are. That's what's at stake in this discussion.[1]

Stephen J. Patterson, another noted *Thomas* scholar, comments similarly:

> [I]f, as many have argued, the Gospel of Thomas is dependent upon the synoptic texts for its traditions, it might be possible to think of Thomas Christianity as a small and relatively insignificant spur, diverging from the main stream of the Jesus movement—a "perver-

sion" of the Jesus tradition, whose more original, and
hence more authentic voice is to be heard in the synoptic texts themselves. On the other hand, if the Gospel
of Thomas is not dependent upon the synoptic gospels,
but rather has its own roots, which reach deeply into
the fertile soil of early Christian tradition, tapping
these sources no less "authentically" than did the
authors responsible for shaping the canonical texts,
then Thomas presents those who wish to think critically about the problem of Christian origins with
something much more important: another point of
view from which to peer down into the murk of earliest
Christianity.[2]

These authorities on the *Gospel of Thomas* make it clear—the
implications of this discussion are significant and potentially far-
reaching.

   Since its discovery the *Gospel of Thomas* has been the subject
of intense study for those with interests in the developments of
earliest Christianity. Scholars have offered a host of mutually
exclusive views on practically every issue; consequently "consensus" is a term rarely used with confidence where the *Gospel of
Thomas* is concerned.[3] Some scholars identify *Thomas* as a document from the late second century,[4] while others date it to the
period between 70 and 80 CE.[5] Competing theories have argued
that *Thomas* was dependent upon the synoptic Gospels,[6] the
Gospel of John,[7] and even the Diatessaron,[8] while others have
argued that *Thomas* was composed independently of the canonical Gospels.[9] It has even been suggested that *Thomas* was source
material for the synoptics.[10] Scholars have variously argued that
Thomas was originally written in Greek,[11] Coptic,[12] and Aramaic
or Syriac.[13] With regard to its genre and theological outlook,
scholars have identified *Thomas* as a Gnostic text,[14] a type of Jewish-Christian wisdom literature,[15] a Jewish-Christian Gospel tradition,[16] an example of Christian mysticism,[17] and an ascetical text

reflecting the views and practices of early Syrian Christianity.[18] It is difficult to imagine a topic of greater importance in the study of early Christianity with less agreement on the most foundational issues.

To make matters worse, those who stand outside academic circles can find these disagreements difficult to process. For the reader unfamiliar with the academic literature, trying to reconcile these views with any success can feel like trying to navigate one's way through a maze. In this book, I aim to help the nonspecialist successfully navigate the maze of *Thomas* scholarship by providing helpful categories in which to place the views of contemporary scholarship. I also aim to present current scholarly views in a clear, fair, and accessible way that both informs readers and allows them to think critically about the important issues involved in discussing the *Gospel of Thomas*. The overview and bibliography provided in this book are intended not to be exhaustive, but rather to serve as a helpful primer for those beginning their study of this important early Christian text. Finally, this book is intended primarily for students, though I hope it will benefit other interested readers as well. Though I have written this book as an entrée into the discussion for those who are not specialists in biblical or early Christian studies, I have included, in the text and in the notes, references to non-English works on the *Gospel of Thomas*. It is my hope that this will not discourage those who are new to the subject but will rather have the opposite effect of encouraging aspiring or future specialists to read more widely on the subject. Having covered preliminary concerns, we begin our study with a brief historical overview.

Discoveries in the Desert

The *Gospel of Thomas* was discovered in December of 1945 when a dozen leather-bound codices were unearthed in the Egyptian desert near Nag Hammadi.[19] While searching for fertilizer, two Egyptian peasants, Muhammad Ali and his brother

Khalifah, discovered a jar containing the manuscripts. After a series of dramatic events, including a family blood feud, the documents were eventually acquired by collectors and transferred to a place where a small group of scholars could examine them.[20] All of the newly discovered documents were preserved in the Sahidic dialect of the Coptic language.[21] In all, the codices contained fifty-two ancient texts, including other "gospels" such as the *Gospel of Philip*, the *Gospel of Truth*, and the *Gospel of the Egyptians*.[22] Unlike these other texts, however, the *Gospel of Thomas* drew instant and widespread attention because it contained many sayings that were similar to and, in some cases, directly parallel to sayings in the canonical Gospel tradition.[23] These similarities immediately raised questions about *Thomas*'s relationship to the canonical Gospels.

To be fair, there are also significant differences between the material contained in the *Gospel of Thomas* and the canonical Gospels. *Thomas* consists of 114 sayings, most of which are attributed to Jesus and nearly half of which were unknown prior to its discovery. Unlike the canonical Gospels, *Thomas* has very little narrative material and contains no account of the passion or resurrection of Jesus. However, for our purposes here, we will focus on the similarities between *Thomas* and the New Testament Gospels, mainly because these form the basis of much scholarly speculation about *Thomas*'s origins.

The history of *Thomas*'s discovery actually begins several decades earlier than 1945. In 1897 and again in 1903, two British archaeologists, B. P. Grenfell and A. S. Hunt, discovered fragments containing previously unknown sayings of Jesus among the Greek papyri found at Oxyrhynchus, another region in the Egyptian desert.[24] Their initial findings were published under the title *Logia Iesou: Sayings of Our Lord*, and a second volume was published in 1904.[25] At the time they were not aware of the source or the significance of these unknown sayings. It was not until 1957, twelve years after the discovery of the Nag Hammadi library, that these fragments were linked to the *Gospel of Thomas*. Examining the Greek fragments against the Coptic text of *Thomas*, the French scholar Henri-Charles Puech found that one scroll (P. Oxy. 1) contained fragments of *Thomas* sayings 26 through 33. A second scroll (P. Oxy. 654) contained fragments of *Thomas*'s incipit[26] through saying 7. A third scroll (P. Oxy. 655) contained fragments of sayings 24 and 36 through 39.[27] With this revelation scholars were now aware of the existence of the *Thomas*-sayings tradition in two languages, Greek and Coptic.

In the years between 1945 and 1958 a handful of scholars trained in Coptic studies, paleography, biblical studies, and other related disciplines studied the *Gospel of Thomas*. Then in 1959 the first English translation of the *Gospel of Thomas* appeared in a volume that came complete with a reconstructed Coptic text.[28] In the wake of this significant new publication, commentaries and theological analyses of the *Gospel of Thomas* began to appear.[29] The history of Thomasine scholarship began in earnest during this period.

The *Gospel of Thomas* has been accessible to the academic world for just over sixty years and to the general public for nearly fifty years. During that period the *Gospel of Thomas* has been subjected to intense scrutiny and has yielded significant disagreement among scholars. To put these debates into perspective it is helpful to look at academic debates over the canonical Gospels. It is true that there are strong disagreements among scholars over numerous issues in the study of these texts. However, there are commentaries on the canonical Gospels that date to a period as early as the late second century, as well as a manuscript tradition that makes the New Testament Gospels the most well-preserved ancient texts in the world. Matthew, Mark, Luke, and John have been in the possession of the church and the academy for nearly two millennia, yielding seemingly endless opportunities for reflection, discussion, and debate. However, the *Gospel of Thomas* has been on the scene for less than a century and boasts only one complete extant copy. Thus, it is all the more astonishing that six brief decades of scholarship on the *Gospel of*

Thomas have witnessed such extreme disagreements and profound paradigm shifts.

Three Crucial Questions

A survey of the history of Thomasine scholarship reveals that early on there was general agreement on three important issues: date, theological outlook, and relationship to the canonical Gospels. Most early scholars held that *Thomas* was a second-century text that was dependent on the synoptic Gospels and reflected a theological viewpoint within second-century Gnosticism. These premises have generally been discussed in connection with one another. When scholars assumed that the document's theological outlook was Gnostic, this conclusion was usually based upon *Thomas*'s presence among a group of supposedly Gnostic texts. The assumption of *Thomas*'s Gnostic outlook colored the perception of scholars who then assumed *Thomas*'s dependence upon the canonical Gospels and in turn assigned to *Thomas* a date somewhere in the mid to late second century. Historically, the connection between these three issues can be demonstrated in the scholarly literature.

This period of general consensus lasted from the late 1950s, when the first commentaries began to appear, to the mid 1980s, when seemingly bedrock assumptions were put to serious question.[30] As this period of scholarly agreement began to erode, a second-century date for *Thomas* could no longer be taken for granted. The assured results of *Thomas*'s dependence upon the canonical Gospels as well as its Gnostic outlook also came under fire. The present period of uncertainty in Thomasine scholarship is where our discussion begins.

The next three chapters will examine current opinion on these three crucial questions. Chapter 2 will examine what scholars are saying about the date of the *Gospel of Thomas*. In other words, how early or how late was *Thomas* composed? Chapter 3 will consider what *Thomas* researchers are saying about the relationship of *Thomas* to the canonical Gospels. Chapter 4 will look at what scholars are saying about *Thomas*'s genre and theological outlook. The book will close with a brief chapter examining *Thomas*'s place in the most recent "quest" for the historical Jesus. We turn now to a consideration of contemporary opinions about *Thomas*'s date.

2
WHAT ARE THEY SAYING ABOUT THE DATE OF *THOMAS*?

As noted in the previous chapter, the earliest wave of scholarship, with a few notable exceptions, regarded the *Gospel of Thomas* as relatively late, generally dating it to the mid-second century CE or later. Initially there were at least two reasons why a later date was proposed. First, the *Gospel of Thomas* was found among fifty other ancient texts, most of which possessed a Gnostic character. Since Christian Gnosticism was a later development, it was simply assumed (rather than demonstrated) that *Thomas* was also late.[1] Second, much of the early scholarship on the *Gospel of Thomas* was undertaken in contexts where the canonical Gospels were given privileged status. Though some scholars were convinced of the primacy of the canonical documents for confessional reasons, the privileging of the canonical tradition may not have been a conscious decision by all early scholars working on this question. Nevertheless, whether for historical, literary, or religious reasons, or because of the conditioned academic views of the time, it was generally assumed that the similarities between *Thomas* and the synoptics should be accounted for by positing *Thomas*'s dependence on the canonical tradition. It goes without saying that these reasons can no longer be taken as "proof" that *Thomas* was composed in the second century. While other texts found at Nag Hammadi have a discernible narrative structure and Gnostic theological views, it is not a given that *Thomas* provides its readers with a Gnostic outlook. In fact, not all of the texts discovered at Nag Hammadi give evidence of the same type of theological system; this is true even of the texts that are regarded as Gnostic by a consensus of scholars.[2] In addition, there are at least two non-Gnostic writings in the Nag Hammadi library—Plato's *Republic* and the *Sentences of Sextus*. This issue will be taken up in greater detail in chapter 4.

Thomas has few narrative elements and no direct theological propositions. Instead, it preserves 114 independent sayings with an ordering that seems to have no discernible logic or structure.[3] Recent scholars have also pursued a much more critical study of literary relationships, raising issues that must be answered before one can confidently assert *Thomas*'s dependence upon the canonical tradition. Since *Thomas*'s Gnostic character and literary dependence upon the synoptics can no longer be assumed, a more detailed argument must now be set forth if one hopes to bolster the case for a second-century date. By and large, recognition of these earlier trends has been a helpful development for *Thomas* studies, if only for the cautionary guidelines it establishes for future scholarly prospects.

Another word of caution needs to be raised at this stage of our discussion. The *Gospel of Thomas*, along with the other literature of the first few Christian centuries, was composed in what was largely an oral culture. In the regions where Christianity developed most rapidly, few people could read and write. Recently scholars have argued that the rate of illiteracy in the near east during this period was somewhere near 85 percent or higher.[4] In addition, scholars have known for a long time that most early Christian storytelling existed in performative, liturgical, and homiletic forms before it ever became fixed in a documentary form. This means that most early followers of Jesus were not able to read for themselves, but rather relied upon a small group of educated individuals to either read to or perform for them.

An awareness of these factors has strong implications for the question of *Thomas*'s date. Questions about the age of a document produced in this setting raise additional questions about ancient literacy, oral performance, textual transmission, communal memory, and other such factors. It also means that any conclusion that intends to be definitive must take into account a set of complex and highly specialized concerns, many of which lie outside the scope of our discussion. Suffice it to say that dating the composition of *Thomas* is a complicated task fraught with uncertainties. Even in light of what can be known with some degree of confidence, conclusions must be held loosely as we await new information from archaeological discoveries, methodological developments, and fresh analyses of ancient texts. With these caveats in mind, we are now in a position to examine the present scholarly views on *Thomas*'s date.

Current opinion on a date for the composition of the *Gospel of Thomas* can be divided into four groups: (1) the view that *Thomas* was composed in the second century; (2) the view that *Thomas* was composed during the same period as the synoptic Gospels; (3) the view that *Thomas* appeared prior to the Gospel of Mark; and (4) the view that various strata can be identified in the *Gospel of Thomas* and assigned to different periods in the development of the sayings tradition. These four approaches are considered below.

The *Gospel of Thomas* as Second-Century Text

Once the dominant position among scholars, the idea that *Thomas* was composed in the mid–second century or later has become a topic of significant debate. In recent years a number of scholars have made passing mention of a probable second-century date for *Thomas*'s composition, but there have been few rigorous attempts to establish this thesis.

Many recent studies have simply assumed *Thomas*'s second-century origin and used that assumption as a basis for reconstruction. Marvin Meyer, recognized for his work on extracanonical

Jesus traditions and his participation in the Jesus Seminar,[5] comments that since "the earliest of the Greek Oxyrhynchus fragments has been assigned a date of around 200 CE, the Gospel of Thomas must have been composed during the second century."[6] Similarly, Bart Ehrman comments that *Thomas*'s "collection—judging from the Gnostic underpinnings of some of his sayings—was probably made sometime in the early second century."[7] Likewise, Darrell L. Bock argues that

> *Thomas* may contain an authentic saying of Jesus here and there, making parts of it early. However, for most scholars, the bulk of it is later, reflecting a *second-century work*. Each saying of *Thomas* has to be assessed on its own terms, but as a whole, *Thomas* is later than Matthew, Mark, and Luke. Efforts to argue it is early as a whole distort the historical record for our first-century sources.[8]

From the foregoing quotations it should be clear that *Thomas*'s second-century origin remains a prominent position among a significant cross-section of scholars, though little argumentation has been offered in recent years to establish this theory.

One recent attempt to situate *Thomas* in the second century is that of Nicholas Perrin. Reviving and reworking a theory earlier espoused by Gilles Quispel[9] and later modified by A. F. J. Klijn,[10] Perrin argues that *Thomas* was dependent on Tatian's Diatessaron, a Syriac harmony of the four canonical Gospels that is generally dated to the 170s CE. For Perrin, this means that *Thomas* is from the *late* second century and also that *Thomas* was originally composed in Syriac. This line of thinking stands against the widely accepted idea that *Thomas* was originally written in Greek and later translated into Coptic. It also runs into the obstacle of dating *Thomas* to the 170s if, as many believe, the Oxyrhynchus texts contain material from the 140s.[11] Perrin is undaunted by these potential difficulties, commenting in several places that scholars rely uncritically on the earlier conclusions of Grenfell and Hunt.[12]

Perrin's dissertation, *Thomas and Tatian*,[13] argues that the *Gospel of Thomas* was originally written in Syriac, and that there is strong evidence that *Thomas* drew from the Diatessaron. Perrin makes his case for *Thomas*'s dependence on the Diatessaron by establishing patterns and keywords in a hypothetical Syriac reconstruction of *Thomas*. His more recent book, *Thomas: The Other Gospel*,[14] is a popularized treatment in which he presents a similar argument in a less technical format.

Perrin builds his case in the latter work by beginning with a critique of important theories in recent *Thomas* scholarship. In the first half of the book, Perrin examines the work of leading *Thomas* scholars Stephen J. Patterson, April D. DeConick, and Elaine Pagels on issues related to *Thomas*'s date, provenance, and composition. He recognizes important contributions made by these three scholars but ultimately regards their theories as insufficient to explain *Thomas*'s origins.

In the second half of the book Perrin restates six questions raised by his three conversation partners and then adds a seventh question of his own. Perrin's answers to these seven questions lead him to the single conclusion of *Thomas*'s dependence upon later Syriac tradition.

The first two questions in his list are:

1. What accounts for the strange sequence of sayings in *Thomas*? Why do the sayings occur in the order they do?
2. How might we explain the ascetical elements in *Thomas*? What socioreligious movement or movements might account for this renunciation of the world?[15]

These questions are raised in Patterson's book, *The Gospel of Thomas and Jesus*.[16] Patterson argues that *Thomas* developed independently of but at the same time as the synoptic Gospels, and that *Thomas*'s sayings reflect a *logoi sophon* ("words of the wise") genre, like the wisdom material found in Proverbs 22—24.[17] This means that *Thomas* is not a later Gnostic text but an early text rooted in the theology of early Christian wisdom literature. Also, Patterson avers that this literature was used by those advocating a life of self-denial (or asceticism). Perrin agrees with Patterson that asceticism is the self-defining feature of the Thomas community, but he rejects Patterson's conclusion that it comes from an early stage of the sayings tradition.

The next set of questions in Perrin's list are:

3. Why is *Thomas* so interested in creational themes, that is, in protology?
4. Why is the *Gospel of Thomas* according to *Thomas*? Why not some other apostle? Furthermore, what does this gospel say about the other apostles and why does it say what it does?[18]

These questions are raised in Elaine Pagels's work.[19] Pagels argues that the communities associated with John and *Thomas* were embroiled in a conflict about the nature of Jesus' message, mission, and identity. This conflict culminated in John's creation of the character now known as "doubting Thomas" to offer a polemic against the *Gospel of Thomas*'s views of Jesus. Perrin rejects this theory and rightly argues that it rests on shaky literary and historical evidence. Specifically, there is no shred of historical evidence for any group of Christians identifying themselves with Thomas as early as 100 CE.

Perrin then asks:

5. What accounts for the disparate substance of the sayings in *Thomas*?
6. Why are all these sayings connected with Jesus,

when Jesus most certainly did not say at least some
of the things attributed to him?[20]

These two questions are raised in the work of April DeConick.[21]
DeConick argues that *Thomas* was the product of a "rolling corpus"
that developed over nearly a century (ca. 30–120 CE). What is now
called the *Gospel of Thomas* began with a "kernel" that likely goes
back to the 30s CE. The original "kernel" went through a number of
accretions until it became fixed in the final form we now possess
(around 120 CE). Perrin saves his strongest critique for DeConick,
raising serious questions about her skepticism over the recovery of
the historical Jesus and her claims regarding orality.[22]

It is worth noting that Perrin regards the previous six questions as valid even though he rejects the explanations Patterson,
Pagels, and DeConick provide to answer them. In order to solid-
ify his case, Perrin adds a final question to the previous six. He
writes:

7. Is there a single setting that can be hypothesized
   behind *Thomas* that answers the above six questions
   in a stroke?[23]

Perrin answers "yes" to this question, concluding that Syrian
Christianity of the late second century is the best context in which
to posit *Thomas*'s emergence. Against that backdrop, he makes his
case for *Thomas*'s dependence on the Diatessaron, its original Syriac composition, and its emergence in the late second century.

This theory has in its favor the widely held belief that
Thomas has a strong connection to early Syrian Christianity.
There is a near consensus among scholars that *Thomas* emerged
in an ascetically-oriented Syrian context. Building on this connection, Perrin goes on to argue for an original Syriac, Diatessaron-
dependent *Thomas* by examining key words and what he calls
"Diatessaronisms" in the Coptic text. He also provides examples
from his own reconstruction of a Syriac *Thomas*.

In the next chapter we will consider in greater detail Perrin's argument for *Thomas*'s dependence upon the Diatessaron. For now, however, it is important to note that Perrin's work follows the pattern that had previously been established in Thomasine scholarship—once the question of dependence or independence has been answered, it leads to inevitable conclusions about date and theological outlook. In a follow-up article from 2006 Perrin writes: "Of course, all these considerations do not *prove* that *Thomas* was written in Syriac, for history never *proves* anything. But what history can do is give a coherent model for explaining the available data. I believe that a Syriac *Gospel of Thomas* carries far more explanatory power than any other model can offer."[24] He goes on to state the implications this hypothesis has for understanding *Thomas*'s sources, sequential development, and date. He writes: "Thomas, our purported informant on the historical Jesus, betrays his source: none other than Tatian's *Diatessaron*. This gives us a *terminus a quo* [earliest possible date] of AD 173 for the *Gospel of Thomas*. It was probably written no later than the end of the second century."[25]

Perrin's work has been subjected to rigorous critique and to date, his views have not achieved a strong following among *Thomas* scholars. Nonetheless, Perrin's insistence that *Thomas* is a compositional unity has offered a formidable challenge to more recent views suggesting *Thomas* is a repository of various Jesus traditions that emerged over time in piecemeal.

Another argument for *Thomas*'s emergence in the second century has recently been proposed by E. E. Popkes. In his monograph, *Das Menschenbild des Thomasevangeliums*, (loosely translated: *The Image of Humanity in the Gospel of Thomas*)[26] Popkes expresses reservations about the possibility of reconstructing the early stages of *Thomas*'s development by locating different layers or stages of tradition. He is especially skeptical about finding material in *Thomas* that goes back to the historical Jesus. Instead, he asserts that *Thomas* is a compositional unity, with close ties to the *Apocryphon of John*. Lexical and conceptual affinities between Coptic *Thomas* and a later Coptic text like the *Apocryphon of John* would be a strong point in favor of a later date—assuming those links could satisfactorily be established. Also, while Perrin finds asceticism in *Thomas*, Popkes avers that *Thomas* reflects a Gnostic theology. Since Gnosticism was a later development, evidence of Gnostic themes and theology also helps Popkes establish a later date for *Thomas's* composition.

Popkes argues that *Thomas's* un-Jewish and even anti-Jewish rhetoric mitigates against an early composition. As with the Epistle of James and the early letters of Paul, the closer a document is to the time of Jesus, the more inherently "Jewish" those documents tend to be. Over time the Jesus movement became predominantly Gentile, which ultimately led to the introduction of non-Jewish thinking and some anti-Jewish sentiment. Popkes sees all of this as pointing away from an early composition for the *Gospel of Thomas*. In the end he concludes that *Thomas* could not have emerged any later than the second half of the second century.

Aside from Perrin and Popkes, few recent scholars have attempted to defend the position that *Thomas* hails from the second century. Nevertheless, that conclusion remains a fixture in scholarly discussions of *Thomas's* emergence. Students beginning their study of the *Gospel of Thomas* should remain aware of this trend and cautiously evaluate unqualified statements about *Thomas's* second-century origin.

The *Gospel of Thomas* Contemporary with the Synoptic Gospels

A second approach to dating the *Gospel of Thomas* argues that the material in *Thomas* is as early as that contained in the synoptic Gospels. Thus, the sayings tradition represented in *Thomas* predates the final formation of the canonical Gospels. This line of thinking has been strongly advocated by Helmut Koester and his students (also known as the Koester school).

There is little question that Helmut Koester represents the most notable exception to the earliest trends in *Thomas* research.

Whereas many earlier studies saw *Thomas* as late and dependent upon the synoptic Gospels, Koester regarded *Thomas* as early and independent. His early works on the question focused on identifying *Thomas*'s genre, date, and provenance.[27] Koester later solidified these views in his book *Ancient Christian Gospels*.[28] There he writes:

> Those who assume that the *Gospel of Thomas* is dependent upon the Gospels of the New Testament have not been able to show that there is any concrete and consistent pattern of *Thomas*'s dependence upon one particular gospel's version of the tradition of the sayings. There is also no trace of the narrative framework into which the sayings are often embedded in the Gospels of the canon. Moreover, a number of studies have shown that in many cases a saying or parable, as it appears in the *Gospel of Thomas* is preserved in a form that is more original than any of its canonical parallels. This means that the tradition of sayings of Jesus preserved in the *Gospel of Thomas* pre-dates the canonical Gospels and rules out the possibility of a dependence upon any of these Gospels.[29]

Koester's case is largely based upon four factors: (1) *Thomas*'s parallels to the sayings source Q—a hypothetical document that is typically dated very early by scholars;[30] (2) *Thomas*'s lack of narrative structure and apocalyptic elements that are found in the canonical Gospels; (3) the presence in *Thomas* of more primitive versions of sayings that also appear in the synoptics; and (4) the "esoteric"—and hence undeveloped—theology we find in *Thomas*.

Stephen J. Patterson, one of Koester's pupils, has also been a strong advocate for this position. Patterson's revised dissertation, *The Gospel of Thomas and Jesus*, is highly regarded among *Thomas* researchers. Patterson's position is that *Thomas* emerged around the same time as the synoptics but developed independently of them. Thus, those responsible for *Thomas*'s composition were drawing from the same pool of Jesus tradition that was available to the synoptic evangelists. Patterson identifies three types of texts in *Thomas*: "synoptic twins" (near parallels), "synoptic siblings" (loose parallels), and "synoptic cousins" (nonparallel texts that have similar form and content).[31] We will examine Patterson's presentation of *Thomas*-synoptic parallels in closer detail in the next chapter. Of concern here is Patterson's assertion that *Thomas* emerged alongside the synoptic Gospels.

Patterson mounts his argument for *Thomas*'s date and provenance along four lines. First, he argues that the collection of sayings found in *Thomas* must come from "a period in which particular communities were still appealing to the authoritative position of particular apostles as a way of guaranteeing the reliability of its traditions."[32] The content of *Gos. Thom.* 12 appeals to the authority of James while *Gos. Thom.* 13 appeals to the authority of Thomas. Patterson argues that this is similar to Matthew's presentation of Peter as an authority figure (cf. Matt 16:13–20). Texts that display this feature, argues Patterson, all derive from the latter decades of the first century CE.

Second, the implied authority of the apostles in *Thomas* is not conferred by virtue of their inclusion among the original Twelve. Rather, it appears that authority is still related to an individual leader's "personal charisma and powers of persuasion, and not yet *apostolic* [authority] properly speaking."[33] Evidence for this assertion is found in saying 13, where Thomas's answer to Jesus' question is deemed adequate while the answers given by Peter and Matthew are inadequate.[34]

Third, the genre of *Thomas* should factor heavily into any discussion of *Thomas*'s date. The *Gospel of Thomas* is a sayings collection, not unlike Q or the collection of parables in Mark 4. Patterson argues that the sayings-collection genre belongs to the earliest period of Christian literary activity. He notes that the "fate of these two examples of the genre [viz., Q or the list of parables in Mark 4] is instructive: neither survived as an independent document; rather, each was absorbed into the more biographical genres favored by Christians in the latter part of the first century."[35]

Finally, in the same way as Koester, Patterson examines *Thomas*'s theology and concludes that it is relatively undeveloped. The strongest point in favor of this argument is the lack of developed christological titles in *Thomas*. Together, these four elements are enough to convince Patterson that *Thomas* was composed during a fairly early period.

In the conclusion to his chapter on *Thomas*'s date and provenance, Patterson writes:

> While the cumulative nature of a sayings collection understandably makes the *Gospel of Thomas* difficult to date with precision, several factors weigh in favor of a date well before the end of the first century: the way which Thomas appeals to the authority of particular prominent figures (Thomas, James) against the competing claims of others (Peter, Matthew); its genre, the sayings collection, which seems to have declined in importance after the emergence of the more biographical and dialogical forms near the end of the first century; and its primitive christology, which seems to presuppose a theological climate more primitive even than the later sayings of the synoptic sayings gospel, Q. Together these factors suggest a date for Thomas in the vicinity of 70–80 CE.[36]

The view espoused by Koester and Patterson has become the leading position among a large segment of North American scholars. For those who regard Q and *Thomas* as representing early strands of the Christian tradition, the Koester/Patterson model has become the most plausible explanation of *Thomas*'s date and provenance.

Thomas Composed Prior to Mark

The idea that the final form of *Thomas* predates the formation of the earliest canonical Gospel (i.e., Mark) has not been a widely accepted position in the history of *Thomas* research. To date, Stevan Davies is the primary recognized proponent of this theory. In his influential book, *The Gospel of Thomas and Christian Wisdom* (1983, 2nd ed. 2005), Davies confidently asserts that *Thomas* should be dated to a period between 50 and 70 CE.[37] In an article from 1992, Davies supports this line of thinking by writing that a "*consensus* is emerging in American scholarship that the *Gospel of Thomas* is a text independent of the Synoptics and that it was compiled in *the mid to late first century*."[38] While Davies's use of the term "consensus" overstates the case, he correctly notes that, at least in North American *Thomas* research, a great number of scholars have moved to embrace such a position.

In 1996 and again in 1997 Davies further developed his understanding of *Thomas*'s date and provenance in two articles aimed at demonstrating "Mark's Use of the *Gospel of Thomas*."[39] Building upon the work of Stephen J. Patterson, Davies mounts a complex argument using form- and redaction-critical criteria. He begins by questioning the theory that *Thomas* drew material from the Gospel of Mark and notes several ways that independent material in *Thomas* could mistakenly appear to have been derived from passages in the synoptics:

1. The scribes who copied *Thomas* likely harmonized elements of Thomasine sayings with the canonical versions with which they were familiar.
2. It is likely that whoever translated *Thomas* from Greek to Coptic did so knowing the sayings as they exist in the canonical Gospels. Thus, some harmonizing is to be expected in Coptic *Thomas*.
3. Coincidence and chance likely played a role. For example, if Luke made a slight change in a saying that he found in Mark, *Thomas* may have coincidentally thought it proper to make the same change in a saying that he found in oral tradition, or oral tradition may have contained that supposed change.

4. In some cases, what appear to be minor redactional changes made by Matthew or Luke may actually reflect the original text of Mark.
5. Redactional material in Luke or Matthew may derive from those authors' knowledge of material in *Thomas*.[40]

Based on this thinking Davies examines thirty-six sayings in the Markan presentation of Jesus' preaching and healing, drawn from Mark 1—8, 11—12 . Of the thirty-six sayings, twenty-one are paralleled in *Thomas*. Focusing upon these twenty-one parallels, Davies attempts to demonstrate that the material found in these Markan units was shaped around logia from the *Gospel of Thomas*. Since Davies is sympathetic to the Koester/Patterson model that views *Thomas* as an example of the *logoi sophon* ("words of the wise") genre, he approaches the discussion with a basic assumption that *Thomas* is relatively early. Against this backdrop he meticulously examines the context, structure, and wording of each parallel unit, finding numerous places where Mark has built a structured narrative around Thomasine sayings. The following list represents material in Mark that Davies argues was drawn from *Thomas*:

Thomas Material Found in Mark

Gospel of Mark	Gospel of Thomas
2:18–22	47, 104
3:20–35	35, 44, 99
4:1–34	5, 6b, 9, 20, 21, 33, 41, 62a
7:14–23	14c, 45b
8:27–33	65, 66
9:35; 10:31, 43–44	4b (POxy 654, 21–27)
11:15–19	64b
11:22–23	48
12:13–17	100

In the conclusion to his second article, Davies introduces three basic facts about the *Gospel of Thomas* that support his argument that *Thomas* was early. He writes:

> First, because of its formal qualities, a barely organized list of sayings, it is presumptively more primitive than any other known compilation of Jesus material. Second, very many of the paralleled sayings in *Thomas* have been less redactionally altered than their counterparts in canonical material, and this includes Q material....Third, the fragments of *Thomas* found at Oxyrhynchus are from an earlier date than are manuscript fragments from most other New Testament writings. These facts do not prove that *Thomas* existed prior to or at least at the time of Mark, but it should give rise to the presumption that it did.[41]

In another place, Davies wonders if *Thomas*'s structure and undeveloped theology together suggest that it predates even the formation of Q![42] Thus, it goes without saying that Davies has an optimism about the early materials in *Thomas* that is not shared by a majority of scholars.

In the end, Davies makes a strong case for some early material in *Thomas,* but this conclusion does not necessarily imply that the entirety of *Thomas* is early, nor does it follow that Mark made use of the *Gospel of Thomas.* The view that *Thomas* predates Mark has a growing number of supporters, though there has not been as much support for the suggestion that Mark used the *Gospel of Thomas.* Nevertheless, Davies' conclusions have provided fertile ground for new discussions to emerge.

Traditions, Layers, and Accretions in *Thomas*

In recent years a growing number of scholars have investigated the emergence of individual sayings in the *Gospel of Thomas* without necessarily speculating on a date for the final form of the text as we now have it.[43] As one might expect these studies also address *Thomas*'s relationship to the synoptics and the sayings tradition that stands behind them. Though this approach has its benefits, the narrow focus of investigation ultimately yields limited conclusions. Nevertheless, scholars are increasingly sensitive to the suggestion that the *Gospel of Thomas* in its final form contains material that is both early (viz., contemporary with the synoptics) and late (viz., from the early second century).

In his commentary, Uwe-Karsten Plisch[44] makes a distinction between two major schools of thought. First, he discusses the predominant "Anglo-Saxon" school, represented by James M. Robinson and Helmut Koester, which sees *Thomas* as very old. He then turns his attention to the dominant German position that was shaped by the influential but tendentious work of Wolfgang Schrage. Schrage regarded *Thomas* as very late and argued that it was dependent upon the synoptics.[45] Plisch contends that Thomasine scholarship is in need of a viable *via media* between these two positions. He writes:

A (sapiential) sayings collection is rather timeless; it neither precludes nor is dependent on the existence of literarily advanced narrative gospels....In terms of transmission, it is obvious that the *Gospel of Thomas* preserved traditions that represent partially an earlier and partially a later time than the synoptic tradition, and it also contains some traditions completely independent of the synoptic gospels. The material compiled in the *Gospel of Thomas* is quite disparate; it comes from various theological traditions. Also the times and locations of its emergence are varied, and it is not possible to put it under one theological umbrella.[46]

Guided by these assumptions, Plisch examines each logion in *Thomas* without assuming an overarching compositional chronology. Practically, this means that *Thomas* can include pre-70 traditions, sayings that conflate or, at the very least, rely on synoptic sayings, and even independent traditions. Given the many uncertainties associated with studying the sayings tradition behind the *Gospel of Thomas*, this view offers *Thomas* scholars an attractive and intellectually honest way of approaching the question of *Thomas*'s date.

The most noteworthy scholarship done on this question in recent years has been that of April D. DeConick. Her work *Recovering the Original Gospel of Thomas*[47] rigorously pursues the question of *Thomas*'s date with an emphasis on the development of traditions contained within *Thomas*. This work (and the companion volume, *The Original Gospel of Thomas in Translation*)[48] represent the most detailed interaction with the question of dating the *Gospel of Thomas* to date. DeConick's thorough knowledge of the Coptic language and her attention to issues such as orality and the theologically complex world of early Christianity have placed her work at the center of most discussions within Thomasine studies. Her work on this question is also noteworthy because she attempts to date *Thomas* by appealing primarily to issues that are *internal* to *Thomas*, rather than appealing to the issue of *Thomas*'s relationship to the canonical tradition—an area where many previous works on this question have failed.

DeConick argues that the *Gospel of Thomas* is the product of a "rolling corpus" that began as an orally transmitted Aramaic core and evolved into the Greek and Coptic texts represented in the final forms that are available to the modern reader. In her analysis, she locates four layers of tradition. The first layer is followed by three successive accretions arising from crises and changes within the communities that were using *Thomas* sayings as authoritative liturgical material.

DeConick refers to the first layer of tradition as the "kernel gospel," which dates to 30–50 CE. According to DeConick's argument the largest grouping of sayings come from that period; notable examples include *Gos. Thom.* 2, 5, 10, 41, 42, 66, 102, and 103. The sayings represented here are essentially apocalyptic in nature and reflect the early Thomasine community's expectation that Jesus would return to bring a decisive apocalyptic judgment. The imminent return of Jesus was an assumption held by many early Christian groups, including those represented in the New Testament canon. DeConick also argues that "the Christological images in the Kernel *Thomas* appear to be most similar to the traditions associated with conservative Christian Judaism from Jerusalem and those developed later by the Ebionites."[49]

According to DeConick there was a gradual shift in the communal ethos that culminated in a second layer of tradition. This material reflects the community's struggle with a changing leadership and is dated to a period between 50 and 60 CE. The examples provided here include *Gos. Thom.* 12 and 68:2.

The third layer of accreted material reveals a change in the community's eschatological expectations. The delay of the Parousia thus gave way to an ideological change in the Thomasine community. This ideological change led to the shift from an eschatological to a mystical understanding of Jesus. Some examples of sayings from this stage are *Gos. Thom.* 3:1–3, 18, 37, 51, 52, and 53. DeConick dates this material to 60–100 CE.

The fourth and final layer DeConick finds is dated to 80–120 CE. This final stage incorporates encratic and hermetic traditions. Encratite Christians were characterized by their strict asceticism (such as the shunning of marriage, the denial of pleasure, and avoidance of intoxicating drinks). The second century Christian, Tatian—recognized primarily for his composition of the Diatessaron—is one of the more well-known encratite figures in early Christianity. The hermetic tradition is associated with Greek and

Egyptian mystical traditions and has often been placed under the category of "Christian Gnosticism" by earlier scholars. The appearance of these two traditions, if it could be established, would obviously argue for a later date for the materials in question. The sayings here are the second largest of the four groupings DeConick proposes. Examples include *Thomas*'s incipit (introductory saying) and *Gos. Thom.* 1, 28, 29, 105, 106, 108, 112, and 114.

A primary thrust of DeConick's argument is that *Thomas* should be "read as a repository of communal memory containing not only early and later traditions but also the reformulations of these traditions based on the contemporary experience of the community."[50] Though her theory is complex and her methodology is not always clearly understood by other *Thomas* researchers,[51] DeConick's work is rarely ignored. Some recent commentators have expressed reservations at attempts to define various stages of composition in the *Gospel of Thomas*.[52] Nevertheless, DeConick's thesis has been engaged by those on all sides of the debate.

In the end, the view that *Thomas* contains a number of different traditions has opened new vistas for assigning a final date for the composition of the *Gospel of Thomas*. Among other things, this view has allowed for an analysis of different sayings without one having to assume a global position about the date of *Thomas*'s final composition.

Conclusion

It should be clear from the foregoing discussion that scholars are nowhere near a consensus on the question of when *Thomas* was composed. Each view presented above takes a segment of the available evidence and attempts to build a convincing case for dating *Thomas*. Because so many factors go into assessing *Thomas*'s date, it is easy to see why there is so little agreement and also why scholars continually appeal to evidence external to the *Gospel of*

Thomas. One of the foundational issues in current discussions about *Thomas*'s date is the question of whether *Thomas* is a compositional unity or a repository of early Christian sayings material. If this question can be answered in a satisfactory way, scholars could likely move closer to a general consensus about when *Thomas* was composed. However, as with nearly every other point of contention in *Thomas* scholarship, it remains to be seen whether such a dialogue can produce a satisfactory answer. We turn our attention now to another contentious discussion—*Thomas*'s relationship to other early Christian literature, specifically the canonical Gospels.

3

WHAT ARE THEY SAYING ABOUT *THOMAS*'S RELATIONSHIP TO THE CANONICAL GOSPELS?

Discerning *Thomas*'s relationship to the canonical Gospels remains one of the most difficult issues within Thomasine studies for a number of reasons. First, discussions of *Thomas*'s relationship to the canonical Gospels tend to be more complex than questions about date or theological outlook. Often form-critical and redaction-critical criteria are used to spell out the relationship between the texts, and this frequently involves detailed arguments about layers of tradition and stratification of sayings material. In many cases, a given reader must have a base of specialized knowledge in order to follow the arguments that are offered for *Thomas*'s dependence on or independence from the canonical tradition.

Second, in the history of scholarship there has been a discernible focus on a predetermined set of related factors, all of which pertain to our earlier discussion of the most prevalent trends in *Thomas* research. When one assumes that *Thomas* is Gnostic or from the second century, it seems clear that *Thomas* preserves a tradition that is dependent on the synoptics. Others argue that *Thomas*, along with Q, represents the earliest genre of Christian literature, and therefore must be independent of the canonical-sayings tradition.

A third reason why this issue has been so difficult to resolve is related to one's opinion of the canonical documents. In many confessional contexts, the canonical Gospels are regarded as the earliest (and hence most reliable) witnesses to the life and vocation of the historical Jesus. This theological assumption has led many to an *a priori* assumption of *Thomas*'s dependence upon the New Testament Gospels with little further investigation. In the judgment of some scholars, the *Gospel of Thomas* contains canonical parallels that appear to be later conflations of synoptic material, as well as other canonical parallels that appear to represent an earlier strand of the Jesus-sayings tradition. Therefore, any theory that attempts to explain *Thomas*'s origins must account for both sets of evidence.

This chapter will look at the various scholarly attempts to situate *Thomas* vis-à-vis the canonical Gospel traditions. We will look first at contemporary arguments about *Thomas*'s relationship to the synoptics. This will be followed by individual discussions of scholarly views on *Thomas*'s relationship to the Gospel of Luke and the Gospel of John. We will then consider the view that *Thomas* is dependent upon the Diatessaron—a document that is itself reliant upon the canonical Gospels. The chapter will close with a brief excursus exploring recent views on *Thomas*'s relationship to Pauline material from the New Testament.

Thomas and the Synoptics

It has already been noted that, with the exception of a handful of scholars, most early attempts to answer the question of *Thomas*'s relationship to the canonical Gospels concluded that *Thomas* was dependent upon the synoptics. For example, in 1961, Bertil Gaertner wrote:

> Characteristic of many of the logia of the *Gospel of Thomas* is the fact that they *combine* different New

Testament sayings of Jesus in a way for which, however, we have no equivalent in the New Testament. For example Logion 14 is a *combination* of sayings from the Sermon on the Mount, Matt. 6, from the Commissioning Discourses, Lk. 10 and Matt. 10, and from the pronouncement on purity and impurity, Mk. 7.15.... The occurrence of these '*compound texts*' in the *Gospel of Thomas* must be treated as one element in a process which can be proved to have been very common during the 2nd and 3rd centuries. Furthermore, we ought to take into consideration that these logia may reflect various attempts at *harmonizing the Gospels*.[1]

Since Gaertner assumed *Thomas* was from the mid to late second century, it made sense for him to argue that the canonical parallels in *Thomas* came about as a result of borrowing and conflating New Testament material. Gaertner's study, like many earlier works which assumed that *Thomas* was from the second century, failed to account for material that appears to have a pre-synoptic origin.

Today most discussions of *Thomas*'s relationship to the synoptics fall into one of two major categories: *Thomas*'s dependence on the synoptics—either directly or through oral transmission, and *Thomas*'s independence from the synoptics.[2] Each view is treated below.

Thomas Dependent on the Synoptics

Published in 1964, the landmark work of Wolfgang Schrage set the tone for an entire generation of German scholarship on the *Gospel of Thomas*.[3] Schrage argued that *Thomas* was dependent on the synoptics, but that dependence was neither literary nor based upon the synoptics in their final forms. Rather, for Schrage, *Thomas* was heavily reliant upon an underlying oral tradition that ultimately found its final expression in the canonical texts.

Overall, Schrage's argument was complex. He approached the question with a general impression that previous studies on the issue were carried out on a basis too narrow to provide a satisfactory answer. Thus, he introduced discussions from form criticism (*Formgeschichte*), tradition criticism (*Traditionsgeschicthe*), and redaction criticism (*Redaktionsgeschicthe*), as well as issues related to textual criticism and Gnostic exegesis. One of Schrage's guiding concerns was to question the scholarly supposition that behind *Thomas* were traces of earlier Aramaic sources as well as a non-synoptic tradition. To address this line of thinking he examined the structure and wording of the Coptic text against the Coptic versions of Matthew and Luke. From this study he concluded that the deviations in style and structure between *Thomas* and the synoptics are generally derived from the Coptic versions of the synoptics. In other words, traces of redaction in Coptic *Thomas* are shown to be dependent upon the redactional activity evident in the Coptic versions of the synoptic Gospels. For Schrage, this means that there is little to no evidence that *Thomas* relied upon a pre-synoptic or Aramaic source for its material. It also indicates that *Thomas* is heavily reliant upon the synoptics in the final Greek forms subsequently rendered into Coptic. Though Schrage's work has been criticized throughout the years, few studies have had such an enduring impact in one segment of *Thomas* scholarship.[4] Among German researchers, Schrage's influence is still felt today.

An example of scholarship that is indebted to Schrage's work, Michael Fieger's revised dissertation also argues for *Thomas*'s dependence upon the synoptic Gospels.[5] Though the bulk of his volume is a detailed commentary on each of *Thomas*'s 114 sayings, Fieger spells out his approach and its underlying assumptions in an eleven-page introduction. Using a redaction-critical methodology, Fieger argues that *Thomas* is an amalgam of material drawn from the synoptics and other sayings material available to Gnostic interpreters of the time.[6] Fieger believes the Gnostic material serves as the interpretive grid through which *Thomas*'s sayings should be read. In other words, synoptic material was co-opted and placed alongside Gnostic material for the explicitly Gnostic theological purposes of the composer(s). Thus, for Fieger, *Thomas* is a thoroughgoing Gnostic work that hails from the second century and relies heavily upon the synoptic Gospels.

Christopher Tuckett has also been a consistent advocate for the position that many sayings in the *Gospel of Thomas* are derived from the synoptic Gospels. In a number of studies published between 1988 and 1998,[7] Tuckett has explored different questions surrounding the relationship between the synoptics and *Thomas*. In an article simply titled, "Thomas and the Synoptics,"[8] Tuckett presents a complex and detailed argument dealing with the two-source theory, the nature of Q, Matthean and Lukan redactional activity, and redaction in *Thomas*, all with a view to demonstrating that *Thomas* was dependent upon the synoptics, and principally the Gospel of Mark. In the second half of that article, Tuckett concentrates his attention on locating synoptic influences in sayings 5, 9, 16, 20, and 55. From this study he concludes that there are numerous instances in which the *Gospel of Thomas* agrees with redacted material found in the Synoptics.[9] He closes the article by commenting that

> The above analysis has shown that there are a number of places where Th shows agreement with elements which are probably redactional in the synoptic gospels. Moreover, Th shows links with material that is due to the redactional activity of all three synoptic evangelists. It would be tempting to deduce from this that Th is dependent on the synoptics *in toto*....[However] each logion must be tested on its own merits....Nevertheless, the fact that Th sometimes shows parallels with redactional material in the synoptics indicates that there is a measure of dependence between our version(s) of Th and our synoptic gospels. At the very least, that should prevent us from making any sweep-

ing generalisations about Th's independence and from making further deductions based on such a theory.[10]

In another article specifically aimed at responding to the arguments of Helmut Koester,[11] Tuckett accuses Koester of fallacious reasoning in his deductions about *Thomas* and Q. Koester regards *Thomas* and Q as examples of the earliest genre of Christian literary activity and has consistently argued that Q and *Thomas* together represent traces of an early "wisdom" gospel. In his treatment of forty-six Q-*Thomas* parallels, Koester finds that *Thomas* often preserves a more original form of the saying. In response to these findings, Tuckett accuses Koester of "perilously circular" reasoning.[12] Koester argues that *Thomas* shows strong links with Q material, but according to Tuckett, he appears to assume rather than clearly demonstrate this conclusion in a number of instances. In the end, Tuckett rejects Koester's wisdom-gospel hypothesis as "unconvincing," concluding that, "we do find a widespread evidence of dependence on the finished synoptic gospels that seems to be too deep-seated to be explained simply by scribal glosses in the later textual tradition of the text of GTh."[13]

Whereas his first article aimed to show *Thomas*'s primary dependence on Mark, Tuckett's second essay is concerned to demonstrate evidence of *Thomas*'s dependence on Matthean and Lukan redaction.[14] Together these two studies constitute a comprehensive argument for *Thomas*'s incorporation of redactional evidence from all three synoptics—a point that argues heavily in favor of Thomasine dependence. In other words, if it can be demonstrated that *Thomas* shows traces of redaction from the synoptic Gospels, this strongly suggests that *Thomas* borrowed from the synoptics.

The scholars examined in this section appeal to similar arguments while also incorporating other strands of evidence. While these various presentations are not likely to generate a consensus on this issue anytime in the near future, it should be noted that many European scholars remain convinced of *Thomas*'s dependence on the synoptic tradition in some form.

Thomas Independent of the Synoptics

It would not be an exaggeration to describe the work of Helmut Koester as foundational to nearly sixty years of North American scholarship on the *Gospel of Thomas*. Just as Schrage's influence can still be detected throughout the German academy, so too can Koester's impact be felt in North America, and particularly in the United States. Many scholars who argue for *Thomas*'s independence from the synoptic tradition can trace their views back to some argument Koester has advanced. This is not to suggest that there is a consensus on this issue among North American *Thomas* scholars, only that those who come down on the side of *Thomas*'s independence are indebted to Koester's scholarship.

It has already been mentioned that Koester regards both *Thomas* and Q as examples of the earliest genre of Christian literature. While Q remains a hypothetical scholarly construct, it is an important element in most contemporary discussions of the synoptic problem. It is safe to say that a majority of scholars working on the synoptics appeal to Q in some form—written, oral, or some combination of both. Thus, the fact that there is no independent evidence for Q is not considered problematic for Koester's proposals.

In the previous chapter we examined Koester's case for assigning an early date to *Thomas*. Since his views on *Thomas*'s date, genre, theological outlook, and relationship to the synoptics are so intertwined, the four elements of his argument bear repeating here. First, Koester argues that *Thomas* and the sayings source Q are two examples of the earliest genre of Christian literature. Both documents consist of a list of sayings without a discernible logic, and both show evidence of an underlying wisdom gospel that was likely transmitted orally. Second, *Thomas* lacks a narrative structure and many of the overtly apocalyptic elements that are present in the canonical Gospels. Thus, *Thomas* is not interested in a futuristic eschatology—a later development in Christian reflection and theologizing—but in providing the reader with a theological perspective rooted in the present. This observation is related to a third point: Koester believes that *Thomas* has an esoteric and undeveloped theology, unlike what we see in the New Testament and in Christian and Gnostic texts from the second century. These three arguments support Koester's analysis of the text of *Thomas*, where he concludes that *Thomas* contains many sayings that appear to be more primitive versions of sayings that also appear in the synoptic Gospels. One may not agree with all the elements of Koester's argument, but his importance in the discussion cannot be denied.

Departing from the dominant strand in German scholarship, Thomas Zöckler also argues that the *Gospel of Thomas* developed independently of the synoptics.[15] Zöckler undertakes a careful study of Q-*Thomas* parallels and concludes that the sayings in Q show more evidence of redaction than those in *Thomas*. He goes on to argue that *Thomas* is likely derived from material that can be dated very near to the source material used in the New Testament, if not earlier. Zöckler finds in *Thomas* no focus on a futuristic eschatology and argues that material traditionally labeled "Gnostic" is actually closer to Jewish wisdom traditions (similar to material in, e.g., Prov 1:23–25). Overall, Zöckler's study intends to address an important issue—*Thomas*'s relationship to the canonical Gospels and the implications this has for our knowledge about the historical Jesus. His conclusions about *Thomas*'s independence lead inevitably to the assertion that the *Gospel of Thomas* is an important early source for historical-Jesus research.

Like Koester, Stephen J. Patterson has also argued that *Thomas* and Q represent the earliest genre of Christian literary activity. In his monograph, *The Gospel of Thomas and Jesus*, Patterson compares material in *Thomas* with the synoptics and identifies three groupings of material: "synoptic twins," "synoptic siblings," and "synoptic cousins."[16] Patterson defines "synoptic twins," the most important parallels, in the following way:

> *Synoptic twins* are sayings in Thomas which have very close parallels in the synoptic gospels. They are like twins, however, in that though their similarities are such that one may be sure they derive from a common origin, their differences reveal that, proceeding from a common point of departure, each version has developed in ways that are unique.[17]

These texts provide Patterson with the most secure basis to argue for *Thomas*'s independence from the synoptic tradition. He argues that these texts, which are the closest to the synoptic Gospels of any texts in *Thomas*, are from the same tradition history as the synoptics but display tendencies and developments that are demonstrably unique. It naturally follows that if the closest parallels are shown to be unique, the less secure parallels can demonstrate this to an even greater degree. Patterson proceeds to provide a detailed commentary of synoptic twins with a view to establishing his thesis that *Thomas* is independent of the synoptics.

In addition to his categorization of *Thomas*-synoptic parallels, Patterson also finds in *Thomas* over seventy Coptic catchwords that have appeared during the process of translating *Thomas* from the original Greek into Coptic. He regards these catchwords as the "organizing principle" behind the *Gospel of Thomas*. Though many will have been "washed away over the course of its transmission history,"[18] there are still a remarkable number of catchwords in the extant Coptic text. This is yet another factor that helps Patterson establish the uniqueness of *Thomas*'s content and structure.

Patterson also follows Koester in arguing that "while Thomas and the synoptic texts do in fact share a large body of material, there is neither a consistent pattern of dependence of one text upon the other, nor a substantial amount of agreement in the way each text has ordered the material they share."[19] In places where *Thomas* seems to include elements of Matthean or Lukan style and redaction, Patterson prefers to see these as examples of later harmonization during the process of textual transmission. In these cases he prefers the term "autonomous tradition" to "independence."[20]

In an article from 2002,[21] Charles Hedrick briefly outlines four scholarly positions on the value of the *Gospel of Thomas*, followed by a fifth alternative of his own: (1) *Thomas* is dependent on the canonical Gospels and should be disregarded as a source for studying Jesus; (2) *Thomas* is independent and therefore a valuable source for studying Jesus; (3) *Thomas* is completely irrelevant for studying Jesus; (4) certain passages in Luke reflect a Thomasine influence and therefore, Luke postdates and is to some degree dependent on *Thomas*. Hedrick follows with his own view:

> My own position is that because the *Gospel of Thomas* contains traditional material not found in the canonical gospels, each saying must be regarded potentially as independent of the canonical gospels, until each individually can be shown to be dependent on the canonical gospels.[22]

Essentially, Hedrick argues that the onus of proof lies with the one who would argue for *Thomas*'s dependence upon the canonical Gospels. This "independent-until-proven-dependent" approach ultimately helps Hedrick avoid the reality that the burden of proof lies with anyone who makes an affirmative declaration. Nevertheless, his novel "anecdotal" approach should be considered, if for no other reason than it departs from most attempts to argue that *Thomas* is independent of the synoptic Gospels.

In the second part of the essay, Hedrick uses saying 82 as a test case for his theory. He asserts that each *Thomas* saying should be examined individually in order to discern whether it has originated from sources other than the synoptics. Tracing evidence from Origen, Didymus the Blind of Alexandria, a fourth-century Armenian text, "Exposition of the Gospel," and the *Gospel of the Savior*, Hedrick aims to show that *Thomas* saying 82 is the result of a long and varied tradition history. What was eventually preserved in *Thomas* as saying 82 was a traditional saying that evolved and was incorporated in numerous literary contexts. Presumably, Hedrick hopes his model will be applied to each logion in the *Gospel of Thomas*. Until then, he contends, it is illegitimate for scholars to assert *Thomas*'s dependence on the synoptics.

Just as many European scholars remain convinced of *Thomas*'s dependence on the synoptic Gospels, many North American scholars argue for *Thomas*'s independence. Though there are a handful of exceptions on both sides of the Atlantic, "stalemate" is probably the best term to describe the state of this question among the two groups of scholars.

Thomas and the Gospel of Luke

At least two recent attempts have been made to argue that the *Gospel of Thomas* had a direct influence on the development of passages in Luke's Gospel. In a short study entitled, "Influence of Thomas Christianity on Luke 12:14 and 5:39,"[23] Gregory Riley locates examples of awkward vocabulary and style that he believes point toward Luke's use of material from the *Gospel of Thomas*. Specifically, he sees Luke's use of the word "divider" (Greek: *meristēs*) in 12:14, as unnecessarily awkward in the context of Luke's emphasis. On the contrary, he contends, the parallel version of this saying in *Gos. Thom.* 72, makes the term "divider" (Coptic: *pōshe*) "the very point of the saying. Within the theology of the *Gospel of Thomas* the denial of a [sic] being a 'divider' is significant indeed."[24] For Riley, this is a clear example of Luke's reliance upon *Thomas*'s version of this saying.

Riley's second example comes from Luke 5:39 / *Gos. Thom.* 47. He argues that the version of this saying in *Thomas* draws from material in Mark that was subsequently adapted to fit *Thomas*'s thematic perspective. According to his analysis, Luke knew *both* the Markan and Thomasine versions and conflated them in his account. Riley concludes:

> These examples show, as it seems to me, that the community of Thomas was in conversation with other Christian groups in the first century and became a source of influence on them and their literary products, the canonical gospels. Several other examples of probable and possible influence of Thomas Christianity on the gospels may be adduced.[25]

This conclusion has led Riley and others to a series of investigations aimed at unearthing Thomasine influence on or points of contact with other canonical material.[26]

Steven R. Johnson has published several articles in which he attempts to demonstrate Lukan and Johannine dependence on specific *Thomas* sayings.[27] He has even devoted an entire book to the consideration of a saying that appears in Mark, *Thomas*, Q, and Luke.[28] In an argument that is as complex as it is speculative,[29] Johnson traces the transmission history of the "Treasure in Heaven" saying (*Gos. Thom.* 76:3 and parallels) and argues that *Thomas*, Mark, and Q were all independently reliant upon an original archetype. Parallels in James 5:2–3 and Matthew 6:19–20 were built upon the Q version while parallels in Colossians 3:1–2 and John 6:27 were built upon the Thomasine version. Luke's version of the saying represents a conflation of material from Q, Mark, and *Thomas*, and retains specific redactional elements of *Thomas*'s version.[30] As with Riley, Johnson believes his study has provided a foundation for future scholarly investigation of *Thomas*'s individual logia vis-à-vis their canonical parallels.[31]

Simon Gathercole has attempted to answer the evidence marshaled by Riley and Johnson in a recent article entitled, "Luke in the *Gospel of Thomas*."[32] Gathercole's examination locates places in *Thomas* where Lukan redaction is present while evidence of Markan redaction is absent. If *Thomas* is thought to be contemporaneous with and independent of Mark (as some scholars have argued), this evidence would suggest that *Thomas* was directly dependent upon a tradition that was not only later than Mark but made extensive use of Markan material. Gathercole considers twelve potential instances in which *Thomas* has been influenced by Luke:

Gos. Thom. 5:2	Luke 8:17
Gos. Thom. 31:1	Luke 4:24
Gos. Thom. 65–66	Luke 20:9–17
Gos. Thom. 33:2–3	Luke 11:33
Gos. Thom. 99	Luke 8:20–21
Gos. Thom. 104	Luke 5:33–35
Gos. Thom. 100	Luke 20:22–24
Gos. Thom. 26	Luke 6:42
Gos. Thom. 47:3–5	Luke 5:36–39
Gos. Thom. 72	Luke 12:13–14
Gos. Thom. 76:3	Luke 12:33

Though he argues that *Thomas* "constitutes an interesting chapter in the reception-history of Luke,"[33] Gathercole is characteristically cautious, concluding that Lukan influence upon *Thomas* is "very probably *indirect*."[34]

While scholars are continuing to explore the possible relationship between Luke and *Thomas*, comparatively little has been written in this area. The Luke-*Thomas* relationship is one area of scholarship that is presently begging for greater clarity.

Thomas and the Gospel of John

Thomas Dependent on John

Discussions about the relationship between the *Gospel of Thomas* and the Gospel of John have not been as frequent in the history of *Thomas* research. In 1962 Raymond Brown published the first full-length article examining the relationship between *Thomas* and the Fourth Gospel.[35] Brown dealt extensively with the language and images of the Coptic *Gospel of Thomas* against the Greek version of the Fourth Gospel. Brown observed that the literature generated to that point on the *Gospel of Thomas* had failed to address the very important question of the relationship between the two works. Citing this lacuna as his motivation for writing, Brown went on to survey fifty-five sayings from the *Gospel of Thomas* that appeared to have verbal, conceptual, or theological parallels with the Fourth Gospel. From there he attempted to elucidate further the relationship between the two works. He concluded that the Johannine parallels in the *Gospel of Thomas* were evidence of *Thomas*'s dependence upon the Fourth Gospel, but that dependence, he argued, was not direct. Instead, he postulated that the *Gospel of Thomas* was influenced by Johannine teaching through at least one and possibly more "Gnostic, incipiently Gnostic, or semi-Gnostic" intermediaries.[36]

In the early years after the publication of Brown's article, little was written on the relationship between *Thomas* and the Fourth Gospel, though several writers did affirm or expand Brown's original thesis. In a 1969 article devoted to text-critical issues in Thomas, Miroslav Marcovich concluded by writing that "the [*Gospel of Thomas*] was inspired by John, as R. E. Brown has shown, and probably to an extent even greater than he recognized."[37] Using Brown's article as his starting point, Jesse Sell published an article in 1980, building largely upon his own 1976 dissertation, in which he argued that there were eight sayings in Thomas that revealed a dependence upon the Fourth Gospel.[38] Sell, however, went a step beyond Brown in arguing for *Thomas*'s direct dependence upon the Gospel of John. He wrote, "I am convinced that knowledge of much of the Johannine tradition was almost certainly one of the many factors which influenced the development of the text of *GT*...I find echoes of fifty-three separate verses from seventeen different chapters of John, strongly reflected in these eight sections of *GT*."[39] Still, by the late 1980s, no serious rebuttal of Brown or treatment of the evidence he surveyed was attempted. However, in recent years, there has been a great shift in thinking among a segment of scholars as the issue of *Thomas*'s relationship to John has taken center stage in *Thomas* research.

John Responds to *Thomas*:
The Community-Conflict Hypothesis

A recent discussion within *Thomas* studies has focused on the suggestion that the Gospel of John was written as a theological response to the *Gospel of Thomas* or to the sayings tradition that stands behind it. The discussion of an intra-Christian conflict involving the communities associated with John and *Thomas* has occupied a handful of American scholars over the last decade and a half. It has been suggested that portions of the Fourth Gospel were written in response to *Thomas* or the theology of the Thomasine community. The scholars most associated with this argument are Gregory J. Riley, April DeConick, and Elaine Pagels.

Gregory Riley's book *Resurrection Reconsidered*[40] is a revised version of his dissertation written under Helmut Koester. Riley concentrates on what he regards as competing views of the resurrection, attempting to demonstrate that the *Gospel of Thomas* refutes the idea of the bodily resurrection of Jesus as well as the eschatological bodily resurrection of Jesus' followers.[41] This is countered, he argues, by the Fourth Gospel's emphasis on the bodily resurrection of both Jesus and his followers. The outward teaching on bodily resurrection in the Gospel of John is therefore, for Riley, a direct response to this glaring error in the *Gospel of Thomas*. He argues further that in the Fourth Gospel, Thomas is consistently portrayed in a negative light—the clearest example of this characterization occurring in the resurrection narrative (i.e., the "doubting Thomas" passage of John 20). This overall characterization, he says, reveals a Johannine polemic against the figure Thomas and the flawed resurrection theology embraced by the Thomasine community. Riley concludes that the two communities "were in close spiritual proximity to one another" and in continual dialogue about their differing theological perspectives.[42] This, he writes, accounts for both the similarities and the differences found in their respective theologies.

For Riley, the Fourth Gospel directs a polemic against two main characters: John the Baptist and Thomas. He sees the presentation of John the Baptist in John's Gospel as a symbol of the conflict between the followers of John and the proto-orthodox followers of Jesus. In the same way, "doubting Thomas" is a character created by John and reveals a theological conflict between the Johannine Christians and the Thomas Christians.[43] The supposed "anti-Baptist" polemic of the Fourth Gospel has been discussed for some time, but for Riley, John the Baptist and Thomas are the two paradigmatic characters placed strategically in key locations of the Fourth Gospel for polemical purposes.

One of the enigmatic passages Riley addresses is saying 71: "Jesus said, 'I will destroy this house and no one will be able to rebuild it.'" There are parallels to this saying in the canonical tradition, and Riley interprets the differences between the *Thomas* saying and the Johannine parallel in light of the conflict he envisions.[44] Riley makes note of the similarities and differences that appear in the parallel temple saying in John 2:19: "Jesus answered them, 'Destroy this temple and I will raise it in three days.'"

In both versions the saying is attributed to Jesus. However, in John 2:19 the "destroyers" are "the Jews" to whom Jesus is speaking; this is in contrast to the *Thomas* version where Jesus himself is the "destroyer." Another difference is found in the use of the word "house" in *Thomas* in place of "temple" in John. A third important difference between the texts is the missing reference to "three days" in the *Thomas* version. Riley interprets these similarities and differences in the two versions as evidence of an ongoing dispute in the sayings tradition over the idea of literal bodily resurrection. He writes:

Jesus is the destroyer in *Thomas*. Again, this is the heart of the revolutionary charge, and the central hazardous point. John, in allowing Jesus to utter the saying, changed the role of destroyer from Jesus to 'the Jews': Jesus tells the Jewish authorities to destroy the temple. *Thomas* allows Jesus to claim directly that he will destroy. This again points to a non-literal meaning for the saying.[45]

Riley contends that a Jesus-saying related to the expectation of Jesus' bodily resurrection began to circulate in early Christian circles; subsequently, Thomas Christians, in an effort to deny the bodily resurrection of Jesus, altered that saying to reflect the Thomasine idea of a spiritual resurrection. Then, the Johannine tradition constructed the figure of Thomas to attack this idea explicitly, while also addressing it implicitly in texts like John 2:19. Thus, for Riley, the Fourth Gospel shows an awareness of *Thomas*'s theology and more importantly responds to and attempts to counter teachings in the *Thomas*-sayings tradition.

In an essay published in 1997,[46] April DeConick mounts an argument similar to the one advanced in Riley's dissertation. DeConick regards the Johannine characterization of Thomas as a "fool," a "dunce," and a faithless individual, which she argues is suggestive of a conflict between the communities associated with *Thomas* and John. This perspective is outlined more fully in DeConick's 2001 essay, "John Rivals Thomas: From Community Conflict to Gospel Narrative."[47] There she wrote that the fourth evangelist's "criticism of Thomas specifically among the disciples is probably not arbitrary given the fact the Gospel of Thomas promotes a type of vision mysticism....[I]t is likely that [the fourth evangelist's] stories about Thomas are dramatizations of an actual dialogue in which the Johannine Community was engaged with the Thomas group."[48] In another monograph, DeConick devotes significant space to exegetical considerations of Johannine and Thomasine texts with a view to raising further questions about the relationship between these two gospels.[49] As with Riley's view, DeConick sees Thomas's appearance in the narrative as evidence of John's polemical stance against the sayings tradition behind the *Gospel of Thomas*.

While DeConick disagrees with Riley's characterization of the conflict between the two communities as focused on resurrection, she nevertheless asserts a real conflict between the two.[50] For DeConick, the root of the conflict (or "discursive field" of their dispute) is soteriological.[51] Specifically, she argues that the Fourth Gospel directs a polemic against a *Thomas* tradition that promotes the idea of disciples seeking visions through ecstatic ascent. This is, she writes, at odds with the Johannine teaching on the necessity of faith apart from sight and is clear evidence of John's response to the *Thomas*-sayings tradition.

DeConick argues that a knowledge of mystical traditions stood behind sayings 15, 27, 37, 50, 59, 83, and 84 of the *Gospel of Thomas*. Specifically, saying 59 is paradigmatic for DeConick: "Jesus said, 'Look at the Living One while you are alive lest you die and seek to see Him and are unable to do so.'" She writes that this saying reflects a premortem experience that "may anticipate death or an eschatological journey but which must be achieved in the believer's lifetime."[52] She sees four specific passages in the Fourth Gospel as direct condemnations of this element in *Thomas*'s theology. Specifically, John 1:18 ("No one has ever seen God."), 3:13 ("No one has ascended into heaven except he who descended from heaven...."), 5:37 ("The Father who sent me has himself witnessed concerning me; you have never heard his voice nor seen him...."), and 6:46 ("No one has seen the Father except the one who is from the Father; he has seen the Father.") are seen as representing explicit polemical responses to this aspect of *Thomas*'s theology.[53]

Much like Riley, DeConick sees the culmination of John's anti-Thomas polemic in the negative characterization of Thomas in the Fourth Gospel. The basis for DeConick's conclusions can be found on the lips of the Johannine Jesus at John 20:29, "Blessed are they who *have not seen* and *yet have believed*"—a clear response, she argues, to Thomas's declaration that seeing is believing.[54]

Elaine Pagels's place in the broader discussion of developments within early Christianity extends further back than Riley or DeConick, though her specific emphasis on John and *Thomas* is more recent. Though some of her recent publications focus specifically on the relationship between the *Gospel of Thomas* and the Gospel of John, Pagels has been generating important works based upon theories of early Christian conflict for more than twenty-five years. In 1979, she published the acclaimed work *The Gnostic Gospels*, where she argued at length that many intra-Christian conflicts can be detected when one examines the Nag Hammadi literature against the writings of the New Testament.[55] She found that much early Christian literature, both Gnostic and orthodox, was replete with polemics directed at other Christian sects that held differing theological views. In some of her more recent work, Pagels builds upon this thinking and shares some of the important conclusions that are found in the works of both Riley and DeConick on the supposed John-Thomas conflict. Specifically, she applies her understanding of multiform expressions of Christianity to the relationship between the *Gospel of Thomas* and the Fourth Gospel and finds a conflict between the two groups rooted in a different interpretation of Genesis 1.

In a 1999 article, she expands upon the community conflict envisioned by Riley and DeConick by finding yet another area of anti-Thomas sentiment in the Fourth Gospel. She sees a Johannine polemic against Thomas Christianity that is rooted in competing views of the creation narrative.[56] According to Pagels, the overall message of *Thomas* is rooted in its underlying exegetical approach to the creation narrative. The prologue of John's Gospel, she argues, is a polemical response to *Thomas*'s incorrect (by Johannine standards) theological understanding of Genesis 1. She writes:

> We do not know, of course, whether or not John actually read the text we call the *Gospel of Thomas*; but

comparison of the Johannine prologue with the above-
mentioned cluster of Thomas sayings suggests that he
knew—and thoroughly disagreed with—the type of
exegesis offered in Thomas. As we suggest, John's
author not only was aware of this clash of traditions
but actively engaged in polemic against specific patterns of Genesis exegesis he intended his prologue to
refute.[57]

For Pagels, John takes issue with *Thomas*'s theological understanding of Genesis 1 and especially *Thomas*'s exegesis of the creation narrative. Like Riley and DeConick, her view puts the two
gospels (and the two communities that stand behind them) in
fundamental theological disagreement with each other.

Pagels finds references to the Genesis creation account in
Thomas-sayings 4, 11, 18, 19, 37, 49, 50, 77, 83, 84, and 85.[58] She
also finds allusions in sayings 22, 24, 61, and 70.[59] Her coverage of
the topic proceeds through a number of the above sayings in an
effort to provide a comprehensive look at *Thomas*'s exegesis of
Genesis 1.

Basing her approach upon the assumption that the *Gospel of
Thomas* has a carefully ordered arrangement, she begins with the
promise in *Thomas*'s first logion ("…whoever finds the meaning
of these sayings will not taste death.") and proceeds to draw out
Thomas's systematic—though not syllogistic—teaching on the
restoration of creation.[60] Further, her exegesis is specifically rooted
in a view that *Thomas* intends readers to pursue a baptismal ritual
that will restore the initiate to a form of Adamic paradise.[61] After
systematically examining the various references to the Genesis
creation narrative in *Thomas*, she concludes:

> Our evidence suggests, then, that Thomas's theology
> and anthropology do not depend upon some presup-
> posed, generic "gnostic myth." Instead, as Schenke pre-
> viously suggested and subsequent research has

confirmed, the source of this religious conviction is, quite simply, exegesis of Genesis 1—and, as we have seen, exegesis that follows a pattern widely known and varied in the ancient world. Such exegesis connects the *eikon* of Gen 1:26–27 with the primordial light (or: light/*anthropos* of Gen 1:3), to show that the divine image implanted at creation enables humankind to find—by means of baptism—the way back to its origin in the mystery of primordial creation.[62]

These conclusions provide her with the basis upon which to claim that John's Prologue represents a polemic against Genesis exegesis adopted by the community associated with Thomas.

Although it is not evident in her discussion of Genesis exegesis in John and *Thomas*, Pagels agrees with Riley and DeConick on the explicit literary evidence of John's anti-Thomas polemic. In her 2003 bestseller *Beyond Belief*,[63] Pagels develops her portrait of the community conflict in forty-three pages, concluding with a discussion of Thomas's negative characterization in John.[64] She concludes that "John may have felt some satisfaction writing this scene [i.e., the "doubting Thomas" passage]; for here he shows Thomas giving up his search for experiential truth—his 'unbelief'—to confess what John sees as the truth of his Gospel: the message would not be lost on Thomas Christians."[65]

While differing on specific issues in their respective presentations, Riley, DeConick, and Pagels agree on several fundamental points: (1) the communities associated with Thomas and John were embroiled in disputes over the person and message of Jesus; (2) these disputes are evident in the polemical stance of the Fourth Gospel toward some elements of *Thomas*'s teaching; (3) at least part of the Fourth Gospel was written in response to certain elements of *Thomas*'s theology; and (4) this anti-Thomas polemic is most clearly seen in the negative portrayal of Thomas in the Fourth Gospel. This final point represents the clearest and most important evidence of John's anti-Thomas polemic, though each scholar makes a sustained case for other evidence in the Fourth Gospel. In the end the case for a John-*Thomas* conflict cannot be made apart from each scholar's view on the role of Thomas in the Fourth Gospel.

Responses to the Community-Conflict Hypothesis

The most comprehensive scholarly work engaging this theory has been that of Ismo Dunderberg. In a series of articles[66] that subsequently became the basis for his book, *The Beloved Disciple in Conflict?*,[67] Dunderberg drew together the arguments of Riley, DeConick, and Pagels and attempted to provide a comprehensive answer to the question of *Thomas*'s relationship to the Fourth Gospel.

In his analysis Dunderberg shows concern for historical issues and for the presentation of characters similar to John's "Beloved Disciple" in other ancient texts. He concludes first by pointing out that the inability of Riley, DeConick, and Pagels to agree on the nature of the John-*Thomas* conflict is problematic for their overall theory.[68] His most convincing point relates to the similarly negative presentation of other characters in the Gospel of John. He writes:

> [T]he proponents of the conflict theory have not taken seriously enough the negative picture drawn of the other followers of Jesus in John. It would be overreaching to see refuted theological positions and other early Christian groups lurking behind every follower of Jesus to whom the author of John has attached some negative features (Nicodemus, Martha, Philip, Thomas, Peter, Judas, etc.).[69]

In my own monograph, I have recently argued that a narrative-critical approach to characterization in the Gospel of John can help to resolve some of the issues raised by Riley, DeConick, and

Pagels.[70] Since the community-conflict hypothesis is based largely upon the Fourth Gospel's characterization of Thomas, a systematic examination of other characters in John can test the theory. Using a historically informed narrative approach, the monograph examines Johannine disciples (Thomas, Peter, Philip, Andrew, Judas [not Iscariot] and the disciples as a representative group) and nondisciples (Nicodemus, the Samaritan woman, Mary and Martha), and finds the community-conflict hypothesis unconvincing. With respect to Riley, DeConick, and Pagels, I conclude:

> Their approach forsakes a great deal of the Fourth Gospel's content and ultimately robs the Johannine narrative of the opportunity to say anything affirmative, declarative, or genuinely didactic to the Johannine reader. The practical outworking of their theory leads to the inevitable conclusion that John's story of Jesus is simply a vehicle for polemic and apologetic in the wider context of theological bickering. However, questions that are raised of Thomas must necessarily be raised of other characters in the narrative, and this is where the community-conflict hypothesis fails. A closer examination of the Gospel reveals a spate of similarly uncomprehending characters, several of whom carry greater theological and narratival significance than Thomas.[71]

Apart from Dunderberg and Skinner, little has been written in response to the community-conflict hypothesis. Outside of a small cadre of influential American scholars, there has not been much support for the supposition that the Gospel of John was written in response to the theology of *Thomas*. It remains a new and relatively unexplored discussion within Thomasine studies.

Thomas and the Diatessaron

As discussed in the previous chapter, Nicholas Perrin[72] has recently revisited and thoroughly reworked a theory first proposed in 1975 by Gilles Quispel.[73] Perrin argues that the *Gospel of Thomas* was originally written in Syriac in the late second century and that the original composition borrowed heavily from the Diatessaron. Building on the insights of scholars who have previously located "catchwords" in the *Gospel of Thomas*, Perrin finds 269 catchwords in the Coptic text, 263 catchwords in a hypothetical Greek text, and an amazing 502 catchwords in his own reconstruction of a Syriac *Thomas*. These catchwords ultimately serve as the basis for an entire theory that posits *Thomas*'s original composition in Syriac, reliance upon the Diatessaron, and emergence in the late second century.

Perrin disagrees with the common opinion that the *Gospel of Thomas* is a random compilation of sayings that shows little evidence of a coherent structure. Instead, he seeks to establish the thesis that *Thomas* is intentionally structured by a string of catchwords that unifies the whole document. Perrin's understanding of what constitutes a catchword is straightforward. He writes:

> I begin with a simple definition: a catchword is any word which can semantically, etymologically, or phonologically be associated with another word found in an adjacent logion. These three categories are essentially the same ones established by Aristotle in his discussion of rhetorical techniques and serve well as a general description of the different types of catchwords.[74]

Then, in nearly a hundred pages, Perrin tabulates and compares catchwords that appear in the Coptic, and hypothetical Greek and Syriac texts. This comparison leads him to conclude:

Upon comparing catchwords as detected in the extant Coptic GT, a hypothetical Greek text, and a hypothetical Syriac text, the quantitative evidence points decisively in the direction of Syriac composition. Whereas previous scholars have theorized a Syriac origin for isolated phrases or even whole sayings, here the results suggest a single linguistic background for the entire collection.[75]

The most obvious weakness in Perrin's overall presentation is the highly speculative nature of the entire enterprise. There is no extant evidence for a Syriac *Gospel of Thomas*, so Perrin is forced to rely upon scholarly opinion about *Thomas*'s Syrian provenance. From there he reconstructs *Thomas* in Syriac, and on the basis of catchwords argues that *Thomas* must have been composed in Syriac. Perrin then argues that there is a high likelihood that a Syriac *Gospel of Thomas* made use of the Diatessaron. The question of method is an important one for examining Perrin's approach and his conclusions. For his part, Perrin is aware of the potential pitfalls of his approach, and he anticipates the criticisms that will arise. Because the number of Syriac catchwords is so much higher than other proposed catchwords, some have accused Perrin of simply finding that for which he is searching. Another question Perrin's thesis fails to address is why the *Gospel of Thomas* seemingly contains no Johannine material from Tatian.

Despite Perrin's claim that his model holds greater "explanatory power" than other approaches,[76] his thesis has not garnered widespread acceptance among a majority of *Thomas* scholars.[77] Nevertheless, Perrin has raised some important questions for both *Thomas* scholarship and Diatessaron studies that must be addressed. For that reason alone, his thesis continues to receive critical engagement and interaction within contemporary scholarship.

Excursus: *Thomas* and Paul

Though this chapter has been dedicated to a discussion of *Thomas*'s relationship to the canonical Gospels, it is appropriate to address a burgeoning area of interest for scholars—*Thomas*'s relationship to the Pauline material in the New Testament. Within *Thomas* studies, rarely has much attention been given to the potential relationship between the *Gospel of Thomas* and the Pauline literature of the New Testament. *Thomas* scholars have had little to say about the possibilities of a genetic relationship between Paul and *Thomas*, and Pauline scholars have virtually ignored *Thomas* altogether. However, several recent studies have brought this question to the surface, giving rise to the hope that a new area of investigation will soon emerge.

Though admittedly rare, suggestions about a Paul-*Thomas* relationship have not been completely absent from *Thomas* scholarship. In an article from 1969,[78] Peter Nagel discussed a possible Paul-*Thomas* parallel when he commented on Paul's use of Leviticus 18:5 and Deuteronomy 30:12–14 in Romans 10:5–8. Nagel noted similar terminology and themes in saying 3 of the *Gospel of Thomas*. He then identified four changes that Paul made in incorporating these texts into his argument: (1) Paul has replaced the Deuteronomic phrase "between heaven and *beyond* the sea" with the dichotomy "in heaven"/"*in* the abyss"; (2) In Deuteronomy 30, attempting to obtain the command from heaven or beyond the sea is futile, while for Paul, these questions are refuted in light of the consequences that would result from them; (3) Paul adds the benefit that one is blessed through confession and belief, an element missing from Deuteronomy 30; and (4) Paul wants to connect "confess" with the mouth and "believe" with the heart.[79]

Following these observations Nagel examined the similar use of Deuteronomy 30 in *Gospel of Thomas* 3 and notes that certain elements peculiar to Paul's use of this Old Testament tradition are also present in the *Thomas* logion.[80] Specifically and most importantly, *Thomas* also changes Deuteronomy's "*beyond* the sea" to "*in* the sea." For Nagel, the presence of this change in both *Thomas* and Romans, and its absence in all other extant versions of the saying, means that Paul and *Thomas* share a common tradition. He concludes that *Gospel of Thomas* 3 is an older version of the parallel saying, adding that the Thomasine text must have been in Paul's consciousness when he wrote his letter to the Romans.

In an article from 1991 entitled, "Paul and the Jesus Tradition," Stephen J. Patterson revisits the question of Paul's relationship to Jesus and the various gospel traditions. He concludes that *Gospel of Thomas* 17 represents a pre-Pauline tradition, and he offers the following unqualified assertion:

> [I]n 1 Corinthians 2 he [scil., Paul] uses the wisdom style of these opponents to compose his own "wisdom speech" (2:6–16), only to correct their views with a few well-placed Pauline twists. Interestingly, in the midst of this speech *Paul quotes a saying from the Gospel of Thomas*....The version of the saying quoted here by Paul is not paralleled word-for-word in *Thomas*, but reflects the sort of differences one would expect to have resulted from oral transmission.[81]

For Patterson, there is at least one instance where a direct relationship between Paul and *Thomas* can be established.

Christopher Tuckett, in an essay from 2003,[82] also takes up the question of a possible relationship between 1 Corinthians 2:9 and the similar logion in the *Gospel of Thomas* 17. His essay examines the similarities and differences, opining that it is very unlikely that Paul would make such substantive changes to a received tradition that supposedly originated with Jesus. Tuckett concludes that there is no evidence for the suggestion that Paul knew this saying as a saying of Jesus. Therefore, *Gospel of Thomas* 17 "represents a secondary development of the tradition compared with the version which Paul gives in 1 Corinthians 2:9."[83]

As one might expect, even an issue as relatively untouched by scholarship as the Paul-*Thomas* relationship has the potential to generate vastly different and even mutually exclusive conclusions. While the studies discussed above have a narrow scope or make only passing mention of possible parallel passages in the writings of Paul and the *Gospel of Thomas*, three recent essays have placed focused attention on a *Thomas*-Paul relationship by examining specific texts, contexts, images, and theological ideas.

In a study entitled, "The Influence of Paul on the *Gospel of Thomas*,"[84] Simon Gathercole attempts to draw a connection between three Pauline passages and similar texts in the *Gospel of Thomas*. Gathercole finds points of contact between Romans 2:25–32 and *Gospel of Thomas* 5, 1 Corinthians 2:9 and *Gospel of Thomas* saying 17, and Romans 10:7 and *Gospel of Thomas* 3. The argument of the essay is driven by a focus on philological and contextual similarities. Gathercole concludes that traditions contained in the *Gospel of Thomas* show knowledge of Paul's writings and a reworking of "Pauline language for un-*Pauline* ends."[85]

Picking up on Gathercole's suggestion that Paul influenced *Thomas*, I argue that his thesis can be taken further. In an article entitled, "The *Gospel of Thomas's* Rejection of Paul's Theological Ideas,"[86] I have sought to advance the idea that the composer(s) of *Thomas* were not only familiar with Pauline texts—either as a result of oral transmission or in written form—but also reworked Pauline texts as a way of expressing this "rejection." The evidence I survey suggests that *Thomas* knew and reworked at least six different Pauline passages.[87] In the end I conclude that *Thomas* consciously used and reworked Pauline texts in a way that would communicate a rejection of Pauline theological ideas:

> [I]t seems clear that at least some elements of *Thomas's* theology developed later and on a much different trajectory than that of Paul. When the authors of the *Gospel of Thomas* found a given Pauline term, phrase, image, or discussion acceptable for use, they also invariably

altered the received Pauline tradition to fit a uniquely Thomasine theological perspective. The authors of the *Gospel of Thomas* were familiar with certain Pauline ideas but ultimately rejected them as having any legitimacy for explaining the ongoing significance of identifying with Jesus through confession.[88]

Taking a different approach from that employed by Gathercole and Skinner (and arriving at different conclusions), Joshua Jipp[89] notes that scholars have made numerous random assertions about the relationship between theological themes in 1 Corinthians and the *Gospel of Thomas*, but no one has attempted to draw them together. Jipp examines a set of similar themes from Paul and *Thomas*. In particular, both emphasize death as a fundamental human predicament, both construct a soteriology that centers upon a death-defeating transformation, and both wind up with implications for bodily practices. At the end of his investigation Jipp finds that while there are similarities, the two traditions are not necessarily in dialogue with one another. He concludes:

> If it is the case that *Thomas* is aware of Pauline texts and traditions, he is remarkably disinterested in *direct conversation* with, or polemic against, Paul's legacy despite their overwhelmingly different constructions of the human predicament, salvation, and bodily practices.[90]

This relatively new interest within *Thomas* studies has the potential to spark a new trajectory within contemporary scholarship. The studies mentioned here anticipate future scholarly prospects for the study of *Thomas*'s relationship to the Pauline corpus. While the connections between *Thomas* and Paul are not as obvious as *Thomas*-synoptic parallels, there are enough points of contact to pique the interests of those within the realm of *Thomas* scholarship.

Conclusion

How is *Thomas* related to the writings of the New Testament in general and the canonical Gospels in particular? The answers we have explored in this chapter range from *Thomas*'s partial dependence on the New Testament to *Thomas*'s independence from the New Testament to the use of *Thomas* by both the synoptics and Paul. As in the case of dating *Thomas*, scholars incorporate numerous external factors in their considerations with the result that a number of mutually exclusive views emerge. Of the three major areas explored in this book (date, relationship to the New Testament, and theological outlook) this one continues to be the most contentious and offers the fewest prospects for scholarly consensus. We turn now to a discussion of *Thomas*'s theological outlook and how it has been understood by contemporary scholars.

4

WHAT ARE THEY SAYING ABOUT *THOMAS*'S THEOLOGICAL OUTLOOK?

In 1992, Boudewijn Dehandschutter concluded his article, "Recent Research on the Gospel of Thomas," lamenting that the "theology of 'Thomas' is often neglected."[1] Over the last decade and a half, this lacuna seems to have been filled as questions about *Thomas*'s theological outlook have generated a number of important studies arriving at very different conclusions.

Generally speaking, most early researchers regarded *Thomas* as a Gnostic text,[2] though Quispel[3] and Koester[4] both offered formidable challenges to that conclusion. The supposition that *Thomas* was Gnostic seems to have been based, in large part, on its discovery among a group of mostly Gnostic texts. Though some have questioned the earlier consensus, it has been somewhat difficult for *Thomas* to shake the "Gnostic" label, especially in popular discourse.

Among those who challenge the old consensus, at least two issues have contributed to doubts about *Thomas*'s Gnostic outlook. First, that *Thomas* was used by Gnostics is not necessarily an indication of its thoroughgoing Gnostic character. This conclusion is supported by the presence of other non-Gnostic texts in the Nag Hammadi library. A growing number of recent commentators have recognized that while *Thomas* may contain some Gnostic traditions or, at the very least, ideas that would have been attractive to second-century Gnostics, this does not in itself constitute a Gnostic outlook.[5] In recognition of this trend, Stevan Davies has commented that Gnostic interpreters used "a range of scripture from Genesis to the Psalms to Homer, from the Synoptics to John to the letters of Paul."[6] Interpreters of *Thomas* must remain aware of the syncretistic proclivities of early Gnostics and evaluate *Thomas's* theological outlook against that backdrop.

Second, the nebulous and elusive definition of "Gnosticism" in the late first and early second centuries has also been an obstacle to identifying *Thomas* as a Gnostic text.[7] Scholars have argued that encratic, hermetic, and other ascetic traditions previously identified as "Gnostic" have been improperly categorized. Suffice it to say that if one still wishes to argue that *Thomas* is a Gnostic document, one must make a more careful and qualified case.

Current scholarship on the question of *Thomas's* theological outlook has arrived at five major proposals: Gnosticism, wisdom, asceticism, mysticism, and Platonism. Because these five categories are not necessarily mutually exclusive, it is difficult to discuss them all individually without referring to at least one of the others. In what follows, we will examine Gnosticism and wisdom together since they have often been discussed in connection with one another in contemporary scholarship. Then we will examine the remaining three views individually, drawing the appropriate connections where necessary.

Gnosticism and Wisdom in *Thomas*

Early researchers tried to identify the specific type of Gnosticism found in the *Gospel of Thomas*. For some, *Thomas* represented Valentinian Gnosticism,[8] while others saw a connection with Naassene Gnosticism.[9] This speculation ultimately gave way to a general theory about *Thomas* representing a garden-variety form of Gnostic religious expression.[10] At a surface level, this kind of imprecise thinking has dominated popular discussions of the

Gospel of Thomas for decades. As we will see in the following sections, such ambiguity begs for greater clarity, and this is one reason for recent movements away from the Gnostic label. Nevertheless, some scholars remain convinced that *Thomas* is best understood as a Gnostic text.

As discussed in the previous chapter, Michael Fieger's monograph, *Das Thomasevangelium*[11] argues that *Thomas* is a second-century Gnostic gospel largely drawn from the synoptic Gospels and other Gnostic traditions. For Fieger, the Gnostic traditions provide the interpretive grid through which the entire gospel is to be read. Some have criticized Fieger's approach as circular. Since he reads every logion in *Thomas* through the lens of Gnosticism, this results in Gnostic interpretations that further reinforce his premise that *Thomas* is Gnostic. In his review of Fieger's monograph, Stephen Patterson criticizes the book's approach, suggesting that a large number of Fieger's Gnostic readings are not demanded by the text but are imposed by the Gnostic grid with which he begins.[12] Patterson's critique echoes an assertion that is commonly voiced by scholars today—for one to interpret *Thomas* as a Gnostic document, one must import Gnosticism into the text. Patterson also comments on Fieger's failure to recognize the presence of sapiential (wisdom) material in *Thomas*. How, he asks, have both wisdom traditions and Gnostic traditions come to exist side-by-side in *Thomas*? Fieger's Gnostic model ultimately fails to answer this question.

E. E. Popkes has also recently argued that *Thomas* has a Gnostic perspective.[13] Recognizing an anti-Jewish rhetoric in *Thomas*, Popkes argues that the collection of sayings concentrates primarily on a process of self-discovery that seems to presuppose an underlying, established form of Christian orthodoxy. Another clue to *Thomas*'s Gnostic perspective, he argues, is its location in Nag Hammadi Codex II. This codex serves as something of a larger "canon," within which *Thomas*'s sayings function as a Gnostic interpretation of Jesus' words. Finally, Popkes finds the closest Thomasine parallels in the *Apocryhpon of John* and to a lesser extent, several other texts from the Nag Hammadi library. On the basis of these considerations, *Thomas* is judged to be a derivative Gnostic work of the late second century.

The term *Gnostic* has also appeared in the titles of several books written or edited by Marvin Meyer.[14] One volume in particular includes Meyer's translation of *Thomas*, accompanied by a Gnostic-like interpretation of each saying.[15] However, Meyer actually takes a qualified approach to the issue of *Thomas's* theological outlook, acknowledging: "While the Gospel of Thomas has some features in common with gnostic gospels, it does not seem to fit the definition of Gnosticism...to a significant extent. Thus I prefer to consider the Gospel of Thomas to be a gospel with an incipient gnostic perspective."[16] In other words, Meyer regards the *Gospel of Thomas* as a wisdom gospel with an externally imposed, gnosticizing point of view. Further, he believes that *Thomas* shares ideas and perspectives with other Gnostic literature without displaying specific features of Gnostic ideologies (e.g., theology, mythology, cosmology, etc.). Overall, Meyer affirms what a growing number of scholars seem to be recognizing—the use of *Thomas* by later Gnostics is not enough for scholars to consider it a full-blown Gnostic text.

William Arnal also sees both Gnostic and wisdom material in the *Gospel of Thomas*, though unlike Patterson he regards some of the material in *Thomas* as genuinely rather than incipiently Gnostic. Noting *Thomas's* formal and thematic inconsistencies, Arnal writes,

> In contradistinction to the sapiential stratum, another body of sayings in the *Gospel of Thomas* is characterized by a gnostic orientation, manifested most trenchantly in their invocation of gnostic mythological motifs.... Common thematic dimensions include the notion of becoming "one" [Coptic: *oua*], "single" [Coptic: *ouōt*], or "alone" [Coptic: *monachos*], an apparent reference to primordial unity especially to androgyny; the belief that

the "end" is in fact a return to the beginning; the expression of salvation in terms of the avoidance of death, and with the nomenclature of "living," and of "repose"; the use of the metaphor of consumption to describe one's mortal destruction by the material world; and references to "light," and to drinking from Jesus' mouth.[17]

Arnal regards these Gnostic themes as part of a secondary redaction to an original wisdom-oriented gospel. Thus, through the introduction of genuinely gnostic material, a later interpreter has co-opted the original gospel and pressed it into the service of Gnosticism.

In posing the question, "Is *Thomas* a Gnostic Gospel?,"[18] Antti Marjanen also finds a loose connection between Gnostic and wisdom traditions in *Thomas*. Examining key themes in *Thomas* alongside themes from other early Christian literature (including the Gospel of John, the *Apocryphon of John*, and the *Gospel of Philip*) he writes:

[I]t remains to be seen what *Thomas*' view of the world reveals about its place in early Christian literature, especially with regard to its relationship to Gnosticism. Even though it is clear that Jewish Wisdom traditions have exerted a strong influence on the *Gospel of Thomas*, as regards their views on the visible world there is a notable difference between *Thomas* and Jewish wisdom."[19]

Marjanen's cautious evaluation of this question is rooted in his awareness of the various scholarly definitions given for "wisdom" and "Gnosticism." This thinking becomes clear when he answers the question, "Is *Thomas* Gnostic?" in both the negative and the affirmative.[20]

With regard to the observation that use by Gnostics does not constitute Gnosticism, Robert McL. Wilson[21] also traces earlier scholarship, noting that a handful of others had previously argued that *Thomas* was not an example of thoroughgoing Gnostic thought, though it was used in creative and imaginative ways by later Gnostics. It is safe to say that overall, recent scholarship on the *Gospel of Thomas* appears to be moving away from the conclusion that *Thomas* is an exclusively Gnostic text, while remaining aware of the interest *Thomas* held for later Gnostic interpreters. Further, many scholars see a combination of ideas rooted in both Gnostic and wisdom traditions. Indeed, the predominant opinion among scholars in recent years seems to be that *Thomas* is primarily an example of wisdom literature with some later Gnostic additions.

Wisdom as a genre and theological category had figured prominently in the work of James M. Robinson and Helmut Koester,[22] and continues to wield strong influence within a large segment of *Thomas* scholarship. Stephen Patterson, a student of both Koester and Robinson, has refined their conclusions about *Thomas*'s provenance and theological outlook. Patterson locates both *Thomas* and Q in the larger tradition of Jewish and Hellenistic wisdom literature. Following his teachers, he understands *Thomas* to be an example of the *logoi sophon* ("sayings of the wise") genre. Against that backdrop he argues that the early traditions in *Thomas* and Q were forms of wisdom, though he also recognizes that the final form of *Thomas* has been incorporated into the service of another theological paradigm—some form of Gnosticism. He writes:

> To be sure, *Thomas* does not contain much of the highly complex mythological structure considered to be typical of Christian Gnostic texts of the second century and later. Nonetheless, the rudiments of Gnostic thought are clearly in place: an expression of alienation to a world conceived of as evil; a revealer whose mission it is to disclose to human beings their true identity and origin in another realm; the call to awaken and return to the heavenly realm of their origin. This is

rudimentary Gnosticism. However, one should not therefore view development on the *Thomas* side of the tradition in discontinuity with what we have already observed on the Q side of the tradition, that is, a gradual modulation into speculative wisdom and apocalypticism. The line between speculative wisdom, with its conviction that wisdom and righteousness have disappeared from the world and must now be revealed to faithful souls through Sophia's emissaries—the line between this and Gnosticism such as we have in *Thomas* is broad and fuzzy.[23]

Plisch makes a similar comment, arguing that *Thomas* in its entirety can hardly be regarded as Gnostic. Instead, *Thomas* possesses a tendency of wisdom moving toward Gnosis,[24] a phrase Plisch borrows from Hans-Martin Schenke ("Die Tendenz der Weisheit zur Gnosis").[25] In this way, Plisch, Patterson, Arnal, and Meyer all differentiate between what they see as *Thomas*'s starting point (wisdom) and its eventual dominant interpretive framework (Gnosticism), though each has a different perspective on how the two eventually coalesced in the *Gospel of Thomas*.

Departing from the Gnostic paradigm altogether, Alexei Siverstev argues that *Thomas* represents an early stage in the development of Christian wisdom literature while also addressing *Thomas*'s relationship to Christian Syriac literature from the second and third centuries.[26] It is a strongly held opinion among many scholars that *Thomas* hails from a Syrian background. Siverstev's thesis takes this view seriously but also works from the assumption that *Thomas* is best understood as wisdom material. Thus, he seeks to bridge two seemingly disparate assumptions that are currently operative within Thomasine research. Siverstev identifies *Thomas* as one early stage in a sequential development that ultimately led to a full-blown Christian wisdom literature. He writes:

The *Gospel of Thomas* perfectly fits the theological agenda of early Syriac literature of the second-third centuries C.E., sharing with it not only an overall theological perspective but also technical language and symbolism....If we accept the hypothesis of *Thomas'* early provenance, it gives us a key to understanding what could be labeled "prepersonified wisdom" mythology in early Christianity.[27]

Siverstev is one of a small number of scholars to see wisdom in *Thomas* while disregarding the presence of material that appears to have some connection with Gnosticism.

From our discussion of both wisdom and Gnosticism, it is clear that many scholars see an interplay between the two theological outlooks at work in the *Gospel of Thomas*. A relatively small number of scholars may argue that *Thomas* is exclusively either a wisdom gospel (e.g., Siverstev) or a Gnostic text (e.g., Fieger, Popkes). However, many affirm that both ideas are present, though questions remain and opinions differ as to the origins of both strands of material.

Thomas and Asceticism

Richard Valantasis has perhaps been the strongest advocate for viewing *Thomas* as an ascetical text.[28] Valantasis asserts that some scholars have made too sharp of a distinction between asceticism and Gnosticism. To describe a movement or a set of texts as "ascetical," he contends, is not necessarily to divorce it from Gnostic or other theological persuasions within early Christianity. According to Valantasis:

At the heart of asceticism is the desire to create a new person as a minority person within a larger religious culture. In order to create a new person, there must be a withdrawal from the dominant modes of articulating subjectivity in order to create free space for something else to emerge.[29]

Arguing that the relationship between asceticism (as he understands it) and Gnosticism "eludes precise articulation,"[30] Valantasis locates *Thomas* within the ascetical tradition of early Syrian Christianity (represented chiefly by Encratite Christians like Tatian and Marcion).

Valantasis draws upon a number of elements that have caused earlier commentators to miss out on the dominant ascetical emphases in the *Gospel of Thomas*. First, the ascetical elements in *Thomas* have often been read as a counterpart to Gnostic elements with the result that a false choice was presented—*Thomas* is either ascetical or Gnostic, but not both. On the contrary, it is possible for a document to be both Gnostic and ascetical at the same time. Second, he argues that asceticism has often been primarily and even exclusively associated with negative elements. For Valantasis, the label "ascetical" has been framed too often in limited or negative terms such as the avoidance of wealth, familial relations, certain foods, and sexual pleasures. Instead, he argues that asceticism as a theological category needs to be expanded to include the "positive articulation of the new subjectivity the gospel presents."[31] Focusing on *Thomas*'s positive perspectives that are aimed at generating a new identity, he writes, "This positive understanding of asceticism revolves about the intentional reformation of the self through specific practices. The presence or absence of an agenda to reformulate or refashion the self provides the key to whether (or not) a text is ascetical."[32]

Another unique feature of Valantasis' presentation is that he approaches the *Gospel of Thomas* from a narrative-critical perspective. A foundational assumption of his narrative reading is that *Thomas* can be appreciated by those outside the ideological and temporal settings of the original composer(s). At a practical

level, this means that *Thomas* can be used with benefit by readers
of different theological persuasions. He contends that:

> [T]hese sayings could be used in a variety of organized
> communities: fourth-century monks could have found
> in them rich ascetical teaching; gnostic Christians
> would have found profound esoteric teaching; ortho-
> dox Christians might have thrilled to hear parables
> without allegorical interpretation. Many people in
> many different kinds of communities could, and did,
> read these sayings and interpret them, but they cannot
> be assumed to share one common theology, perspec-
> tive, or even interpretation of the sayings.[33]

Finally, Valantasis sees *Thomas*'s interpretation of Jesus as
one of three dominant conflicting interpretations operative in the
first decade of the second century CE. One interpretation is taken
up by the Johannine perspective, which promulgates the idea of
experiencing the living Jesus through his passion and resurrection. A second interpretation is reflected in the writings of
Ignatius, who promotes an imitation of Jesus within the church
and participation in his death. According to the third interpretation, the "*Thomas* kind of person alone hearkens to the days of
immediate presence of Jesus without any need to engage in either
imitation of Jesus or of the disciples."[34] From the Thomasine perspective, the only necessity for experiencing Jesus is the proper
interpretation of the gospel's sayings. Again, this particular perspective could function within a number of different theological
outlooks and does not necessarily imply a Gnostic outlook or pre-
clude an ascetical outlook.

Risto Uro also sees asceticism in *Thomas*, though he defines
"ascetical" more narrowly than Valantasis. Like Valantasis, however,
Uro points out that Encratism (strict Christian asceticism) and
Gnosticism are not necessarily mutually exclusive categories and
asserts that the "characterizations of the *Gospel of Thomas* as an

'ascetic' or 'encratite' document are in need of refinement."[35] Uro traces the discussion of *Thomas's* theological outlook, attempting to demonstrate that *Thomas* should not be regarded as an Encratite text, though it does show evidence of ascetical elements. Uro's view is that ascetic ideals were common in early Christianity and can be found both in Paul and in later first-century writings, such as the Gospel of Luke and Revelation. Thus, on the scale of ascetical emphasis, *Thomas* is to be situated somewhere between Luke and later apocryphal works such as the *Book of Thomas the Contender*.[36]

With regard to Gnostic themes in *Thomas*, Uro argues that *Thomas* represents a similar cosmological view as that found in the *Dialogue of the Savior*. Both documents have a view of the divine origin of humanity and lack traditions related to a Demiurge (one of the lesser, Gnostic deities responsible for creation). Like his University of Helskini colleague, Antti Marjanen, Uro ultimately contends that a given scholar's definition of Gnosticism dictates, to a large degree, whether or not Gnosticism is found in *Thomas*. Consequently, he does not find the Gnostic label as problematic as many North American scholars do.

Thomas and Mysticism

Over the last decade, April DeConick has distinguished herself as one of the leading authorities within *Thomas* studies. She has written or edited five books[37] and published a number of essays[38] on issues related to the *Gospel of Thomas*. Her conclusions have continually been engaged by scholars across the spectrum of opinion in Thomasine research. Simply stated, if one wishes to be conversant with contemporary *Thomas* scholarship, DeConick's research cannot be ignored. One hallmark of her scholarship has been an attempt to move conversations beyond an impasse that may have been generated by traditional categories, and thereby create new ways of conceiving of the *Gospel of Thomas*. An example of this approach, which has already been discussed in chapter 2, is DeConick's proposal that *Thomas* is a repository of communal memory. This con-clusion is the foundation for her reconstruction of *Thomas's* "rolling corpus," which includes a kernel gospel (30–50 CE) and three layers of accretions (50–120 CE). This discussion has pro-vided an alternative to conversations that rely heavily on a connec-tion between *Thomas* and the canonical Gospels.

Another instance where DeConick's research has moved beyond the dominant categories is her work on *Thomas's* theologi-cal outlook. DeConick insists that *Thomas* cannot and should not be considered Gnostic, but rather what she calls "ascent and vision mysticism."[39] While DeConick does acknowledge that there are Gnostic parallels to some sayings in *Thomas*, she asserts that these parallels arose as a result of *Thomas's* impact on Gnostic traditions rather than vice versa. Taking on the two most prominent theories about *Thomas's* theological outlook (Gnosticism and wisdom), she writes:

> The *Gospel of Thomas* does not represent the voice of some late generic Gnostic heresy or some early unique sapiential Christianity. Rather it is quite cogent with early Syrian Christianity as described in the oldest lit-erature from the area....I am completely convinced that the *Gospel of Thomas* theologically and practically is an infant of eastern Christianity, particularly as it was practiced in Syria. It is one of our earliest, if not our earliest text showcasing a very old form of "Ortho-dox" thought. As such, it is very at home in the Syrian environment and represents old Syrian religiosity. It is a precursor to eastern Orthodoxy, as even a superficial reading of that catechism reveals. Eastern Christianity is about a *mysticism of the heart and the progressive transformation of the soul into its glorious Image.*[40]

DeConick also avers that the mystical traditions she finds in *Thomas* have a theological connection to early apocalyptic thinking. She writes that the "mystical tradition in *Thomas* is very old, and emerges out of connections with apocalyptic thought. Once the eschatological story did not manifest as expected, these Christians remodeled the familiar sayings of Jesus by shifting their focus to the mystical dimension of Jesus' sayings."[41]

Using a methodology that she refers to as "traditio-rhetorical criticism," DeConick attempts to trace how a discourse is ultimately codified into a textualized ideology. Her revised dissertation, *Seek to See Him*[42] examines a number of sayings in the *Gospel of Thomas* (most notably *Gos. Thom.* 50), with a view to arguing that *Thomas* is a mystical text. DeConick builds upon the earlier research of Gilles Quispel, who argued that *Thomas* was influenced by at least three sources—an Encratite source (possibly the *Gospel of the Egyptians*), a Jewish-Christian gospel (possibly the *Gospel of the Nazoreans*), and a hermetic source. While DeConick does not argue for a series of written sources, she nevertheless follows Quispel in the supposition that *Thomas* was influenced and shaped by these traditions. In addition to these three materials, DeConick adds early Jewish mystical traditions like that reflected in Philo, Jewish apocalyptic texts, and material from Qumran. She writes, "This early Jewish mysticism filtered into Christianity, Gnosticism, and the Hekhalot literature, teaching that, after proper preparations, one could seek to ascend into heaven in order to gain heavenly knowledge and a transforming vision of the deity."[43]

In another volume, *Voices of the Mystics*,[44] DeConick uses her traditio-rhetorical approach to examine the emergence of mystical traditions in the Gospels of John and *Thomas*. Against a background study of vision mysticism in the ancient world, DeConick argues that the Fourth Gospel developed a "faith mysticism" meant to serve as a polemical response to the mystical soteriology presented by the *Gospel of Thomas*. She supports this thesis by delving into the texts of early Syrian Christianity and demonstrating that such conversations continue into later periods of Christian development.

DeConick's research on this question has led her to conclude that *Thomas* reflects a trajectory within proto-orthodox Christianity that valued mystical teaching. *Thomas*, she asserts, has been improperly categorized by modern scholars as Gnostic or sapiential "for the simple reason that our categories, particularly in regard to mysticism in this period, could not contain it."[45]

All of the implications of DeConick's proposal have yet to be considered, though the breadth of her research demands that her argument be engaged. She has a strong knowledge of the requisite languages (especially Coptic), presents a wide range of evidence, and immerses her discussion in an array of ancient texts from different ideological backgrounds within early Christianity. Her investigations into *Thomas*'s theological outlook demand that future conversations about *Thomas* and mysticism take place.

Thomas and Platonism

In 1985, Howard Jackson, published a revision of his Claremont dissertation, *The Lion Becomes Man*,[46] in which he explored the possible presence of Platonic ideas in the *Gospel of Thomas*. The monograph focuses specifically on the difficult saying, *Gospel of Thomas* 7: "Jesus said: 'Blessed is the lion that the human will eat so that the lion becomes human, and cursed is the human whom a lion will eat so that the lion becomes human."[47] Jackson argues that the lion image is the central element in this saying and proceeds to trace the background of leontomorphic figures (i.e., figures presented in the form of a lion) in the literature and art of antiquity. After examining Gnostic traditions of a leontomorphic Demiurge and Egyptian images of a leontomorphic creator, Jackson concludes that these are ultimately ancillary to *Gospel of Thomas* 7. Instead, a better source for the lion image in *Thomas* is Platonic anthropology.

According to Plato, the lion symbolizes the soul's *thumos*—a Greek term denoting the spirited and passionate element of the human psyche. Like a lion, the *thumos* needs to be tamed in order to bring the psyche into proper balance and make it subject to human reason. Jackson's discussion also makes reference to the Coptic translation of Plato's *Republic*, one of two non-Gnostic texts found in the Nag Hammadi library. He concludes:

> It is against this background that logion 7 of the *Gospel of Thomas* must be explained. Its lion is the summational representative of all passion, perhaps specifically sexual passion for the ascetics who coined the logion, and if it may be blessed it is not as the leontocephalic creator but rather as his element in man which may nevertheless be redeemed by being obedient to— "devoured" by—his more spiritual master.[48]

Jackson's study, while somewhat dated, provides a solid alternative explanation for one admittedly difficult saying in the *Gospel of Thomas*. However, the limited results of his investigation raise the question of whether Platonic thought can be located elsewhere in *Thomas* or regarded as the philosophical framework from which its author(s) where operating.[49] Is logion 7 an anomalous example of Platonic thought in *Thomas* or is there more to Jackson's thesis? In the last several years Stephen Patterson has tried to answer this question in greater detail.

Long an advocate for seeing wisdom traditions in *Thomas*, Patterson has revisited the question of *Thomas*'s theological outlook, suggesting that *Thomas* is a reading of Jesus through a Platonic lens, particularly the lens of "middle Platonism." Dillon describes middle Platonism as follows:

> [T]he period of Platonism between Antiochus of Ascalon (c. 130–68 B.C.) and Plotinus (A.D. 204–70), characterized by a rejection of the skeptical stance of the New Academy and by a gradual advance, with many individual variations, toward a comprehensive dogmatic position on metaphysical principles.[50]

Philo of Alexandria is perhaps the best known Jewish proponent of middle Platonism. This new direction in Patterson's scholarship appears in nascent form in comments from his 1998 essay, "Understanding the *Gospel of Thomas* Today."[51] There he writes:

> *Thomas* Christians viewed the world as an inferior place. They gave expression to this view in the way they lived and in how they thought. But is there evidence in *Thomas* to indicate that they expressed their disdain for the world in terms of their personal piety as well?...In all its various forms (Gnosticism, Hellenistic Jewish wisdom theology, Jewish mysticism) *this speculative theology contained heavy elements of Platonic (or neo-Platonic) dualism.* That is, those who cultivated these traditions thought of a human being as a mixture of material and spiritual elements. The material part of a person was thought to be connected closely to the material world, and thus subject to the corruption to which the Platonists believed the material world was prone. In this way the material element in a person was considered inferior to the spiritual element, whose origin, by contrast, was believed to lie in the divine godhead itself.[52]

The sort of dualism that some Gnostic and ascetic groups would have found attractive was foundational to those influenced by Platonic thought.

In a more focused study, "Jesus Meets Plato: The Theology of the *Gospel of Thomas* and Middle Platonism,"[53] Patterson develops his thinking along these lines. He begins by examining the emphases of middle Platonic thought and moves on to investigate how and where these emphases are operative in the *Gospel of Thomas.* He looks at middle Platonic ideas about anthropology, the image of God, light, and the relation between motion and rest. In his characteristic manner, Patterson is cautious in his evaluation. He finds elements of Platonic thought in *Thomas* but does not argue that *Thomas* is an example of full-fledged Platonism. In his conclusion he writes:

> Was Thomas a Middle Platonists' Gospel? It would be difficult to say this without much qualification.... At the very least, one must say that *GThom* is a wisdom gospel that has been brushed over with the animating notions of Middle Platonism.... What is clear, however, is that *GThom* works with one of the dominant religious and philosophical schools of its day, Middle Platonism. In this sense, it stands near the beginning of what would become a long tradition of Platonic Christian theology, and is probably our earliest example of such effort.[54]

Because this view is a relative newcomer in Thomasine studies, it remains to be seen if Patterson's proposal will be met with broader acceptance among *Thomas* scholars.

Conclusion

Within most segments of *Thomas* scholarship researchers have expressed an awareness of different theological persuasions at work in the *Gospel of Thomas*. Many current proposals reject the attempt to define its theological outlook in rigid categories. Scholars are no closer to a consensus on the question of *Thomas*'s theological outlook, though there appear to be more points of interaction in this area than in discussions of *Thomas*'s date and relationship to the canonical Gospels. For instance, many scholars recognize some connection between *Thomas* and Gnosticism, even if only that *Thomas* was attractive to later Gnostic interpreters. Others have added greater clarity to the discussion by suggesting that the genre of *Thomas* (a list of sayings) could have made it of considerable interest to groups with many different theological persuasions. The prospects for future scholarly conversation are much greater here than in the two previous areas surveyed in this book.

In our introductory chapter I began by outlining some of the broader implications of *Thomas* research. In recent years, one area of study in which *Thomas* has undergone careful scrutiny has been the academic "quest" for the historical Jesus. Our final chapter will consider *Thomas*'s place in recent historical Jesus studies.

5
THE *GOSPEL OF THOMAS* AND
THE HISTORICAL JESUS

In light of our considerations in the foregoing chapters, it should come as no surprise that scholars are divided over the significance that the *Gospel of Thomas* holds for historical Jesus research. Those who regard *Thomas* as an early text place an unusually high emphasis on its importance for reconstructing the life and vocation of the historical Jesus. Those who regard *Thomas* as late, Gnostic, or both are obviously quite skeptical of its value for researching the historical Jesus. There is not space here for a full-scale discussion of the *Gospel of Thomas* in recent historical Jesus research.[1] That subject could itself serve as the basis for an entire book! The purpose of the present chapter is to examine two prominent and mutually exclusive views that are representative of much contemporary scholarship on the historical Jesus. In the remainder of this chapter, we will look briefly at the role the *Gospel of Thomas* has played in three of the more high-profile historical Jesus projects undertaken in recent years: (1) John Paul Meier's multivolume work, *A Marginal Jew: Rethinking the Historical Jesus*,[2] (2) the Jesus Seminar's volume, *The Five Gospels*,[3] and (3) the scholarly works of John Dominic Crossan, especially *The Historical Jesus: The Life of a Mediterranean Jewish Peasant*.[4]

Overall, Meier's work represents the school of thought that is skeptical of *Thomas's* value for reconstructing elements in the life of the historical Jesus. On the opposite end of the spectrum sits the collaborative work of the Jesus Seminar along with the scholarly works of John Dominic Crossan, one of the Seminar's most prominent members. Together, Crossan and the Jesus Seminar represent the school of thought that regards *Thomas* as a reliable source for historical Jesus research.

John Paul Meier's *A Marginal Jew*

A leading figure among Jesus researchers, John Paul Meier has produced four in a projected five-volume series on the historical Jesus. At the beginning of his first volume, Meier examines a host of noncanonical sources that may or may not be of value in establishing some basic facts about the life and vocation of Jesus. He looks at the writings of Josephus, various other Jewish and pagan writings, extracanonical sayings of Jesus, the apocryphal gospels, and the Nag Hammadi literature. Within this detailed discussion, Meier devotes significant space to an analysis of the *Gospel of Thomas* and its place within historical Jesus research.[5]

For Meier, there are several complicated factors that make it difficult to use *Thomas* as a helpful source for discussing the historical Jesus. First, while *Thomas* may not represent full-blown Gnostic thought, it does contain elements that lean in that direction. Meier comments that only in light of a "strange mixture of mysticism, asceticism, pantheism, and polytheism" can one understand *Thomas*'s enigmatic sayings.[6] He also comments that *Thomas* represents realized eschatology in its most radical form.[7] For Meier, these are indications that *Thomas* likely emerged later than the canonical Gospels. Despite his opinion about *Thomas*'s Gnostic tendencies and emergence in the second century, however, he still wonders if there might be some early Jesus material preserved in *Thomas*.[8]

Five considerations[9] ultimately lead Meier to a negative conclusion about *Thomas*'s usefulness for historical Jesus research:

1. In the material he surveys, Meier sees a trend that leaves him with the impression that most "authentic sayings" of Jesus located by scholars can easily be dismissed as "bizarre examples of Christian imagination run riot."[10]

2. The canonical Gospels both emerge from and generate ongoing oral tradition. Practically, this means that as one moves into the second century it becomes more and more difficult to identify material that has not been influenced by the canonical Gospels.

3. While many argue that *Thomas* represents a shorter and therefore "purer" form of the Jesus tradition, it may be that *Thomas* has reduced material because of a preference for shorter and more mysterious formulations that reflect its proto-Gnostic theology.

4. Many comment on the plentiful *Thomas*-Q parallels, but Meier is struck by the amount of uniquely Matthean and Lukan material found in *Thomas*. He also mentions, approvingly, Raymond Brown's thesis that *Thomas* is to some degree reliant upon Johannine material.

5. Meier argues that *Thomas* appears to eliminate certain elements of redaction from the synoptic accounts while occasionally preserving synoptic order and/or theological tendencies.

After all of this evidence has been considered, Meier concludes that:

> [T]he more probable hypothesis is that the *Gospel of Thomas* knew and used at least some of the canonical Gospels, notably Matthew and Luke. Indeed, if the *Gospel of Thomas* used all Four Gospels, the frequency with which each Gospel is used would roughly mirror

> what we see throughout the rest of the 2d-century
> Christian literature....Thus, rather than diverging
> from the common pattern of 2d-century Christian lit-
> erature, *Thomas* by and large conforms to it.[11]

Meier recognizes that his perspective will not be shared by all historical Jesus researchers. This recognition leads him to "keep one eye on the sayings" in *Thomas* as a "check and control on [his] interpretation of the data in the canonical Gospels."[12] Despite this contrived sensitivity, it is clear that Meier regards *Thomas* as having very little value for recovering genuine histori- cal Jesus material.[13] Consequently, the *Gospel of Thomas* does not factor significantly into the three volumes that have followed his inaugural tome. At the end of the day, Meier's study must be regarded as the most important current historical Jesus project that sees little value in the *Gospel of Thomas*, though it should be noted that many others have arrived at this conclusion.

The Jesus Seminar

A great deal has been written about the impact of the highly controversial Jesus Seminar over the past two decades, much of which does not need to be reviewed here. To be sure, the Jesus Seminar has its detractors as well as its supporters,[14] though it has become nearly impossible to ignore the Seminar's conclusions or the methodology that stands behind them.[15] Unlike Meier, the Jesus Seminar regards the *Gospel of Thomas* as a helpful tool for reconstructing some elements of Jesus' life and ministry; this importance is reflected in the title of their inaugural work, *The Five Gospels*. By now, the methodology of the Jesus Seminar is well known, though it bears repeating here. For nearly a decade, as fel- lows of the Seminar met to discuss the words of Jesus, they placed colored beads into a coffer as they "voted" on whether or not a given saying was authentic. The beads were divided into four colors: red, pink, gray, and black. The colors are explained as follows:

Red: Jesus undoubtedly said this or something
        very like it.
Pink: Jesus probably said something like this.
Gray: Jesus did not say this, but the ideas contained
        in it are close to his own.
Black: Jesus did not say this; it represents the
        perspective or content of a later or different
        tradition.[16]

Fellows of the seminar considered Jesus' words in the four canonical Gospels and the *Gospel of Thomas*, and throughout their considerations they regarded *Thomas* as equal in historical importance to the New Testament Gospels. Robert J. Miller, himself a fellow of the Jesus Seminar, explains:

Thomas received little scholarly attention until quite recently when several new and important studies converged on two conclusions: that Thomas represents an independent tradition and that some of its sayings are as early, or even earlier, than those in the synoptic gospels. Impressed by these findings, the Seminar deemed Thomas to be as worthy of close and careful attention as the New Testament gospels. Scrutinizing the sayings in Thomas one by one over the course of several years has produced general agreement within the Seminar with this new understanding of Thomas.[17]

Against this backdrop, the fellows of the Jesus Seminar ultimately coded thirty-six sayings in the *Gospel of Thomas* as red or pink.[18] This statistic, however, is not as significant as it might seem at first glance. Of the thirty-six sayings, thirty-four have parallels in the synoptics which are also colored pink or red. The remaining two

sayings without synoptic parallels—*Gospel of Thomas* 97 and 98—
are colored pink. Miller goes on to explain the process by which
the Seminar arrived at these conclusions:

> Making this decision about these two parables was not
> easy for the Seminar. Each parable was initially voted
> gray. A later reconsideration met with the same result.
> An unprecedented second reconsideration resulted in
> pink averages for both. If the Seminar is right about
> these fascinating and mysterious parables, these are lit-
> erally "lost" teachings of Jesus, unknown to the world
> for sixteen centuries.[19]

Thus, as a comparative tool, *Thomas* has proven, at least to the satisfaction of a majority of the Seminar's fellows, to contain some
genuine sayings of the historical Jesus.

While the Jesus Seminar has been rightly criticized by many
for some of its methodological flaws, the role of *Thomas* in the
whole enterprise has been somewhat overstated. The *Gospel of
Thomas* served as part of the comparative database for scholarly
consideration, but the Seminar believes that *Thomas* ultimately
tells us very little about what the historical Jesus actually said. For
the fellows of the Jesus Seminar, *Thomas*'s biggest value has been
in providing numerous noncanonical parallels to texts from the
synoptic Gospels. Apart from two unique sayings that *may* have
come from Jesus, the *Gospel of Thomas* has not become the overarching grid through which the Seminar looks at the historical
Jesus. Rather, *Thomas* is one of several valid tools for a more
expansive consideration of Jesus' words. Thus, if we were plotting
points on a spectrum, we might describe the Jesus Seminar as
making moderate use of *Thomas* in reconstructing Jesus' words.
What the Jesus Seminar has done in moderation, one of its most
important members, John Dominic Crossan, has done in much
greater measure.

John Dominic Crossan

Charles L. Quarles has recently written, "Of the scholars who rely heavily on the *Gospel of Thomas* in providing a portrait of the historical Jesus, few have been more prolific or influential than John Dominic Crossan."[20] This is, no doubt, an apt description of the sought-after scholar who has written over a dozen books related to the historical Jesus and ancient Christian texts dealing with Jesus.[21] More than any one individual within historical Jesus studies, Crossan has been an advocate for viewing the *Gospel of Thomas* as one of our earliest Christian documents. His stratification of the earliest Christian-sayings tradition contains a wealth of material from *Thomas*, and he has consistently maintained that *Thomas* dates from the period 50–70 CE—which would make it contemporary with some of the earliest canonical letters (usually dated to the late 40s and early 50s CE) as well as the traditions contained in the Gospel of Mark (which is generally dated to 70 CE).

Crossan's most important work on the historical Jesus is his five-hundred-page volume, *The Historical Jesus: The Life of a Mediterranean Jewish Peasant*. Described on the front cover as "The first comprehensive determination of who Jesus was, what he did, and what he said," *The Historical Jesus* devotes substantial space to ancient sources pertinent to the study of Jesus' life in first-century Palestine. In his chronological stratification of Jesus material, Crossan lists Paul's letters, 1 Thessalonians (ca. 50 CE), Galatians (52–53 CE), 1 Corinthians (53–54 CE), and Romans (55–56 CE), followed by the *Gospel of Thomas* (mid-fifties, CE) as the earliest writings within the Christian tradition. He argues that *Thomas* contains at least two layers of tradition, one that is secondary and likely added in the late 60s to early 70s CE, and one that emerged around the time of Paul's earliest writings. Practically, this means that the earliest material in *Thomas* predates all four canonical Gospels and was emerging around the time that Paul's ministry was flourishing in Asia Minor.

Crossan begins the book with a list of sayings that he believes come from the historical Jesus; contained in that list are a number of sayings from the *Gospel of Thomas*.[22] Later in the book Crossan examines three arguments that will factor heavily into his reconstruction of early texts: (1) Helmut Koester's work on 1 Corinthians 1—4;[23] (2) Stevan Davies on the *Gospel of Thomas*;[24] and (3) John Kloppenborg's reconstruction of Q.[25]

Koester argues that the opponents envisioned in 1 Corinthians (53–54 CE) can be identified as Gnostics or proto-Gnostics. Crossan uses this assertion to argue that there is a sapiential (wisdom) interpretation of Jesus' teachings that clashes with Paul's apocalyptic interpretation, all of which is occurring in the early 50s. Similarly, Davies argues that the *Gospel of Thomas* contains a number of sayings that relate to an apocalyptic understanding of Jesus, and this is opposed by the Thomasine Jesus' sapiential response. So, in each case we have a conflict between apocalyptic and wisdom interpretations of Jesus. Crossan then uses Kloppenborg's study to demonstrate that the apocalyptic and sapiential strands are combined very early in the formation of Q. This diversity, which Crossan argues is all very early, establishes a database that allows *Thomas* to be used with benefit in discussing Jesus. He writes:

> Brought together, these three insightful studies, by Koester on 1 Corinthians 1—4, Davies on the *Gospel of Thomas*, and Kloppenborg on the *Sayings Gospel Q* (that is, in my view, *from three documents of the fifties CE*) indicate that sapiential and apocalyptic understandings of Jesus were both well developed and simultaneously present at an extremely early stage.[26]

The above considerations are only a small portion of what Crossan has written and asserted about *Thomas*'s value over the years. Suffice it to say that his approach, which has also been criticized,[27] has been used to broaden the base of material considered valid for examining the historical Jesus. Though Crossan's optimism about *Thomas*'s value is not shared by all, or even most historical Jesus scholars, his views have gained a significant hearing over the past two decades.

Conclusion

How can such opposing views exist side-by-side in *Thomas* scholarship? If there is one thing this book has sought to emphasize, it is how little agreement there is among those who pursue advanced research on the *Gospel of Thomas*. Even historical Jesus researchers are divided over the significance *Thomas* has for helping to establish authentic Jesus material. As in every other case we have examined here, one must make a determination about *Thomas*'s date, relationship to the New Testament, and theological outlook before one can make a positive assertion about *Thomas*'s place in the modern quest for the historical Jesus. Once these determinations are made, they inevitably lead to other conclusions. In each case—Meier on one end of the spectrum, and Crossan and the Jesus Seminar on the other—conclusions about *Thomas*'s date, theological outlook, and relation to the New Testament significantly impact their conclusions about *Thomas*'s value for historical Jesus research. This consideration of *Thomas* within historical Jesus studies serves to underscore once again how little agreement there is in the academic study of the *Gospel of Thomas* and how the answers to foundational questions inevitably lead to fixed assertions about when, how, and in what context *Thomas* emerged.

CONCLUSION

What are they saying about the *Gospel of Thomas*? Our study has shown that scholars are saying many things about *Thomas*, most of which hinge on three questions: (1) When was *Thomas* composed? (2) How is *Thomas* related to the writings of the New Testament? and (3) What kind of theological outlook is reflected in *Thomas*? We have explored the broad scope of contemporary research on these three questions and established that there is little agreement among scholars on the most fundamental issues in Thomasine studies. All of this raises the question, "What *do* scholars agree about?" We pose this question for one important reason: If scholars can identify areas of common agreement and center future discussions around those areas, it may be possible to establish broader points of consensus in the areas covered by this book.

As I have noted several times throughout my discussion, many scholars believe that *Thomas* has a strong connection to early Syrian Christianity. This point of common agreement could be used as the basis for future conversations. Further explorations into the Syrian Christian context in the first three centuries CE have the potential to provide fodder for fruitful discussions. Also, despite the protestations of a small minority, most scholars agree that *Thomas* was originally written in Greek and is preserved in its earliest extant form in the Oxyrhynchus fragments. Only later was *Thomas* translated into the Coptic version we now have. Taken together, these areas of general agreement have the potential to serve as a helpful basis for fresh examinations of *Thomas*'s date, relationship to the New Testament, and theological outlook. Until we are able to move beyond the traditional categories established in the preceding decades of Thomasine scholarship, we are destined to remain at the current impasse.

GLOSSARY

Asceticism—a religiously based lifestyle characterized by self-denial.

Canonical Gospels—the four gospels of the New Testament; Matthew, Mark, Luke, and John.

Codex—handwritten manuscripts produced in antiquity; often made of papyrus leaves bound togther.

Coptic—the last stage of the Egyptian language prior to the Islamic conquest.

Demiurge—a deity responsible for shaping the material world from a preexisting chaotic condition.

Diatessaron—the first harmony of the four canonical Gospels; written in Syriac by Tatian around 170 CE.

Encratism—Christian ascetic sect from the second century; known for abstaining from meat, intoxicating drink, and sexual pleasure.

Form criticism—critical approach to biblical and extrabiblical literature concerned with identifying different forms of folk literary expression.

Hermeticism—system of religious belief rooted in the pseudepigraphic literature attributed to Hermes Trismegistus.

Incipit—the opening line or first few words of a text; in the *Gospel of Thomas* it reads, "These are the secret sayings which the living Jesus spoke and which Didymos Judas Thomas wrote down."

Logion / logia—a saying / sayings.

Middle Platonism—period of Platonism between Antiochus of Ascalon (ca. 130–68 CE) and Plotinus (204–70 CE), characterized by a rejection of the skeptical stance of the New Academy.

Naassene Gnosticism—a Gnostic sect originating around 100 CE; claimed to have a connection with James the Just through his disciple, Mariamne.

Nag Hammadi—region in upper Egypt now known as Chenoboskion.

Nag Hammadi Codex II (NHC II)—the codex from Nag Hammadi in which the *Gospel of Thomas* is found.

Nag Hammadi library—fifty-two documents discovered in the Egyptian desert near Nag Hammadi in 1945.

Narrative criticism—branch of literary study concerned with the final form of a document.

Oxyrhynchus—region in upper Egypt now known as El-Bahnasa.

Q—short for "*Quelle*" (German: "source"); hypothetical textual source defined as the material Matthew and Luke share that is not found in Mark.

Redaction criticism—critical approach to biblical and extrabiblical literature concerned with how received material has been shaped in the editorial process.

Sahidic—the most prominent dialect of the Coptic language; the dialect in which most extant ancient Coptic texts are preserved.

Source criticism—critical approach to biblical and extrabiblical literature concerned with discerning the sources used in a given document.

Synoptics—the canonical Gospels Matthew, Mark, and Luke.

Syriac—a dialect of Aramaic once spoken throughout the Near East.

Tatian—late second-century apologist responsible for creating the Diatessaron.

Textual criticism—critical approach to biblical and extrabiblical literature concerned with establishing the original text of a document.

Tradition criticism—critical approach to biblical and extrabiblical literature concerned with discerning how traditions passed from oral to written form.

Valentinian Gnosticism—Gnostic sect associated with the second-century figure, Valentinus (ca. 100–160 CE).

NOTES

Chapter 1: The *Gospel of Thomas* in Historical Perspective

1. Stevan Davies, *The Gospel of Thomas and Christian Wisdom*, 2nd ed. (Dublin: Bardic, 2005), ix–x.

2. Stephen J. Patterson, *The Gospel of Thomas and Jesus* (Sonoma, CA: Polebridge, 1993), 9.

3. While consensus is rare, scholars generally agree on an ascetically oriented, Syrian provenance for the *Gospel of Thomas*.

4. A second-century date for *Thomas* was a view held by many researchers on the *Gospel of Thomas*. For instance, Bertil Gaertner, one of the earliest commentators on the *Gospel of Thomas*, writes: "Hitherto there has been a fair measure of agreement over the date AD 140–150, and no one has shown any desire to refer it to any earlier period" (*The Theology of the Gospel According to Thomas*, trans. Eric J. Sharpe [New York: Harper & Brothers, 1961], 271). More recently, Marvin Meyer (*The Gospel of Thomas: The Hidden Sayings of Jesus* [San Francisco: Harper-Collins, 1992], 10) has written: "Since the earliest of the Greek Oxyrhynchus fragments has been assigned a date of around 200 CE, the Gospel of Thomas must have been composed during the second century or even the latter part of the first century CE."

5. See, for instance, Patterson, *The Gospel of Thomas and Jesus*, 113–20.

6. Many early researchers labeled Thomas as a Gnostic or proto-Gnostic source. Among these are: Robert M. Grant and David Noel Freedman, *The Secret Sayings of Jesus* (New York: Doubleday, 1960); R.

McL. Wilson, *Studies in the Gospel of Thomas* (London: Mobray, 1960); Gaertner, *The Theology of the Gospel According to Thomas*; Rodolphe Kasser, *L'Évangile Selon Thomas: Présentation et commentaire théologique,* Bibliothèque Théologique (Neuchatel: Delachaux et Niestlé, 1961); H. E. W. Turner and Hugh Montefiore, *Thomas and the Evangelists* (Naperville, IL: Allenson, 1962); Johannes Leipoldt, *Das Evangelium nach Thomas* (Berlin: Akademie-Verlag, 1967); and Ray Summers, *The Secret Sayings of the Living Jesus: Studies in the Coptic Gospel According to Thomas* (Waco: Word, 1968). There is no longer such widespread agreement about *Thomas*'s theological outlook.

7. Raymond E. Brown, "The Gospel of Thomas and St. John's Gospel," *NTS* 9 (1962): 155–77; Jesse Sell, "Johannine Traditions in Logion 61 of the Gospel of Thomas," *PRSt* 7 (1980): 24–25.

8. Gilles Quispel, *Tatian and the Gospel of Thomas: Studies in the History of the Western Diatessaron* (Leiden: Brill, 1975); idem, "L'Evangile selon Thomas et le Diatessaron," in *Gnostic Studies II* (Istanbul: Nederlands Historisch-Archaelogisch Institut te Istanbul, 1975), 31–55; idem, *Makarius, das Thomasevangelium und das Lied von der Perle* (NovTSup 15; Leiden: Brill, 1967). This line of thinking has also been resurrected in the scholarship of Nicholas Perrin. See Perrin's dissertation, *Thomas and Tatian: The Relationship between the Gospel of Thomas and the Diatessaron* (Atlanta: Society of Biblical Literature, 2002); idem, "Thomas: The Fifth Gospel?" *JETS* 49 (2006): 67–80; idem, *Thomas: The Other Gospel* (Louisville: Westminster John Knox, 2007). Differing slightly from Quispel's original thesis, Perrin posits *Thomas*'s indirect dependence on the synoptics by way of the Syriac Diatessaron. He also argues for an original Syriac version of the *Gospel of Thomas*.

9. See the pertinent sections in Helmut Koester, "ΓΝΩΜΑΙ ΔΙΑΦΟΡΟΙ: The Origin and Nature of Diversification in the History of Early Christianity," *HTR* 58 (1965): 283; idem, "Dialog und Spruchüberlieferung in den gnostischen Texten von Nag Hammadi," *EvT* 39 (1979): 532–56; idem, "Gnostic Writings as Witnesses for the Development of the Sayings Tradition," in *The Rediscovery of Gnosticism: Proceedings of the International Conference on Gnosticism at Yale,* ed. Bentley Layton (Leiden: Brill, 1980). See, also Koester's introductory comments on the *Gospel of Thomas* in the *Nag Hammadi Library in English,* rev. ed. James M. Robinson (San Francisco: HarperCollins, 1988), 124–26. For a more recent and developed treatment, see Helmut Koester, *Ancient Christian*

Gospels: Their History and Development (Philadelphia: Trinity Press International, 1992), 75–124. Here he suggests that the author of the Johannine literature directs a polemic against a number of Jesus traditions located in the *Gospel of Thomas*.

10. Stevan Davies discusses at length Mark's dependence upon the *Gospel of Thomas*. See "Mark's Use of the Gospel of Thomas," *Neot* 30 (1996): 307–34, and a follow-up article coauthored with Kevin Johnson, "Mark's Use of the Gospel of Thomas, Part II" *Neot* 31 (1997): 233–61.

11. While not a true "consensus" position, this view currently enjoys fairly wide acceptance. Most *Thomas* scholars view the Oxyrhynchus fragments as strong evidence of a Greek *Vorlage* (original language) for the *Gospel of Thomas*. Nicholas Perrin, who argues for a Syriac *Vorlage*, is a notable exception to this general trend. See n. 8 above for a list of Perrin's pertinent works on this issue. In his recent commentary, Uwe-Karsten Plisch ignores those who dissent on the issue of compositional language, confidently writing that the "Coptic text of the *Gospel of Thomas* is a translation of a Greek text, just like every other text in Codex II of the Nag Hammadi find. *This is clear* from the fact that only knowledge of the complete Coptic *Gospel of Thomas* made it possible to identify three Greek fragments from a manuscript discovery in the middle-Egyptian town Oxyrhynchos which had already been published a half century prior to the discovery of the Nag Hammadi texts" (*The Gospel of Thomas: Original Text with Commentary,* trans. Gesine Schenke Robinson [Stuttgart: Deutsche Bibelgesellschaft, 2007], 11, emphasis added).

12. G. Garitte, "Les 'Logoi' d'Oxyrhynque sont traduits de copte," *Mus* 73 (1960): 335–49.

13. See, for instance, Antoine Guillamont, "Sémitismes dans les logia de Jésus retrouvés à Nag-Hammâdi," *JA* 246 (1958): 113–23; idem, "Les Sémitismes dans l'Évangile selon Thomas: Essai de classement," in *Studies in Gnosticism and Hellenistic Religions Presented to Gilles Quispel on the Occasion of his 65th Birthday,* ed. R. van den Broeck (Leiden: Brill, 1981); Gilles Quispel "The Gospel of Thomas and the New Testament," *VC* 11 (1957): 189–207; idem, "Some Remarks on the Gospel of Thomas," *NTS* 5 (1959): 276–90; Jan J. W. Drijvers, "Fact and Problems in Early Syriac-Speaking Christianity," *SecCent* 2 (1982): 173–75; Bentley Layton, *The Gnostic Scriptures* (Garden City, NY: Doubleday, 1987), 377; Nicholas Perrin, "NHC II, 2 and the Oxyrhynchus Fragments (P. Oxy 1,

654, 655): Overlooked Evidence for a Syriac *Gospel of Thomas*," *VC* 58 (2004): 138–51.

14. See the works listed in n. 4, above.

15. The influential work of Stevan Davies (*The Gospel of Thomas and Christian Wisdom*) is a good starting point for a serious discussion of this topic. Davies's lucid argumentation offered the first serious alternative to understanding *Thomas* as a Gnostic document. See also the helpful discussion of pertinent issues in Alexei Siverstev's, "The Gospel of Thomas and Early Stages in the Development of the Christian Wisdom Literature," *JECS* 8 (2000): 319–40.

16. Gilles Quispel, "Qumran, John and Jewish Christianity," in *John and the Dead Sea Scrolls,* ed. James H. Charlesworth (New York: Crossroad, 1991), 144–46.

17. See April D. DeConick, *Seek to See Him: Ascent and Vision Mysticism in the Gospel of Thomas,* VCSup 33 (Leiden: Brill, 1996).

18. See Richard Valantasis, "Is the Gospel of Thomas Ascetical? Revisiting an Old Problem with a New Theory," *JECS* 7 (1999): 55–81; idem, *The Gospel of Thomas,* New Testament Readings (London & New York: Routledge, 1997).

19. Nag Hammadi is located in Upper Egypt on the western bank of the Nile and lies just outside the region formerly known as Chenoboskion.

20. For a brief overview of the discovery of the Nag Hammadi Library and the acquisition of these manuscripts by scholars, see James M. Robinson, ed., *The Nag Hammadi Library in English* (San Francisco: HarperSanFrancisco: 1990), 22–26. Robinson goes into greater detail in an essay entitled, "Nag Hammadi: The First Fifty Years," reproduced in Stephen J. Patterson, James M. Robinson, and Hans-Gebhard Bethge, *The Fifth Gospel: The Gospel of Thomas Comes of Age* (Harrisburg, PA: Trinity Press International, 1998), 77–109. Bart D. Ehrman (*Lost Christianities: The Battles for Scripture and the Faiths We Never Knew* [Oxford: Oxford University Press, 2003], 51–54) also provides a helpful overview of the events surrounding the discovery of the Nag Hammadi library.

21. Coptic was the last stage of the Egyptian language prior to the Islamic conquest. Under Islamic rule Arabic was adopted throughout Egypt, and Coptic virtually disappeared as a spoken language, though it remains the liturgical language of the Coptic Orthodox Church.

22. These "gospels" are generally dated by a majority of scholars to the middle of the second century. Each gospel reveals evidence of later theological developments.

23. A unique feature of the *Gospel of Thomas* is that it contains parallels to canonical sayings that appear to be later conflations of synoptic material and some canonical sayings that appear to represent an earlier strand of Jesus sayings–tradition. This is one reason for the ongoing debate about *Thomas*'s antiquity and relationship to the synoptics.

24. Oxyrhynchus (modern El-Bahnasa) is located in Upper Egypt, approximately a hundred miles southwest of the capital city of Cairo.

25. B. P. Grenfell and A. S. Hunt, *Logia Iesou: Sayings of Our Lord* (London: Henry Frowde, 1897); cf. also idem, *New Sayings of Jesus and a Fragment of a Lost Gospel from Oxyrhynchus* (London: Henry Frowde, 1904).

26. The *Gospel of Thomas* begins with the words, "These are the secret sayings that the living Jesus spoke and Didymos Judas Thomas wrote down." Not numbered among the 114 sayings, it generally appears as the introductory formula prior to the first saying.

27. See Puech's detailed study "Une collection des paroles de Jésus récemment retrouvée: L'Évangile selon Thomas," in *Comptes rendus de l'Academie des Inscriptions et Belles Lettres* (Paris: Institut de France: 1957), 146–67.

28. *The Gospel According to Thomas: Coptic Text Established and Translated,* trans. A. Guillamont, H.-Ch. Puech, G. Quispel, W. Till, and Yassah 'Abd Al Masih (Leiden: Brill, 1959).

29. Several notable volumes were published between 1959 and 1962, e.g., Jean Doresse, *L'Évangile selon Thomas* (Paris: Plon & Rocher, 1959); Grant and Freedman, *The Secret Sayings of Jesus* (1960); Wilson, *Studies in the Gospel of Thomas* (1960); Gaertner, *The Theology of the Gospel According to Thomas* (1961); Kasser, *L'Évangile selon Thomas: Présentation et commentaire théologique* (1961); Turner and Montefiore, *Thomas and the Evangelists* (1962).

30. It should be noted that Helmut Koester is a significant exception to this general trend. Koester has consistently argued that the *Gospel of Thomas* represents one of the earliest stages of the sayings tradition; he has also argued that *Thomas* should be given equal weight with the canonical Gospels when discussing the historical Jesus. (See n. 9 above for a list of Koester's important contributions to this discussion.) Koester

was persuaded by the influential work of Walter Bauer, *Orthodoxy and Heresy in Earliest Christianity* (Philadelphia: Fortress, 1979)—originally published in 1932 under the German title *Rechtgläubigketi und Ketzerei im ältesten Christentum*. Bauer argued that Christianity experienced a multiform development in the early centuries after Jesus' crucifixion. He contended that the group that ultimately "won" (viz., the proto-orthodox Christians) established what became Christian orthodoxy. This means that orthodoxy and heresy should not be considered legitimate categories in light of the various expressions of Christianity during the first four centuries CE Bauer's speculative theory gained more credibility among some critical scholars once the Nag Hammadi library was discovered. For his part, Koester regarded the Nag Hammadi discoveries as proof of Bauer's theory.

Chapter 2: What Are They Saying About the Date of *Thomas*?

1. See n. 29 in chapter 1 for an example of this type of thinking among early *Thomas* researchers.

2. Plisch writes, "Nag Hammadi Codex II is neither linguistically nor in terms of content a homogeneous volume. The various tractates are associated with different 'schools.' *Ap. John* and *Hyp. Arch.* belong to the Sethian Gnosis, *Gos. Phil.* Is a Valentinian Christian-Gnostic text, *Gos. Thom.* and *Book Thom.* belong to the Thomas tradition, and *Exeg. Soul* and *Orig. World* are unique texts that cannot be assigned to a particular tradition. The patron of the codex, who we do not know, was obviously interested in a book that comprised a broad range of theological perspectives" (*The Gospel of Thomas*, 11).

3. Helmut Koester has commented that there seems to be no internal logic behind *Thomas*'s ordering of material: "What is most puzzling about the composition of sayings in this wisdom book is the arrangement and order of the sayings. There is seemingly no rhyme or reason for the odd sequence in which the sayings occur in the *Gospel of Thomas*." While some have tried to explain the logic behind the ordering of *Thomas*'s sayings, Koester goes on to say that "several attempts have been made to find the author's compositional principle, [but] none of

them [is] convincing" (*Ancient Christian Gospels*, 81). One of Koester's former students, Elaine Pagels ("Exegesis of Genesis 1 in the Gospels of Thomas and John," *JBL* 118 [1999]: 481), encourages readers to adopt "the hypothesis that the sayings are not randomly arranged, but carefully ordered to lead one through a process of seeing and finding 'the interpretation of these sayings' (log. 1). This is not to suggest, however, that the author follows an obvious or syllogistic rationale." See also Allen Callahan ("'No Rhyme or Reason': The Hidden Logia of the *Gospel of Thomas*," *HTR* 90 [1997]: 411–26), who attempts to demonstrate the author's "compositional principle."

4. For more on this subject, see William V. Harris, *Ancient Literacy* (Cambridge: Harvard University Press, 1989).

5. The Jesus Seminar is discussed at greater length in chapter 5.

6. Meyer, *The Gospel of Thomas: The Hidden Sayings of Jesus*, 10. In the very next phrase Meyer opines that *Thomas* could come from, "the late first century."

7. Bart D. Ehrman, *Jesus, Apocalyptic Prophet of a New Millennium* (Oxford: Oxford University Press, 1999), 75–78.

8. Darrell L. Bock, *The Missing Gospels: Unearthing the Truth Behind Alternative Christianities* (Nashville: Thomas Nelson, 2006), 63 (emphasis added).

9. For a representative sample of his work, see Gilles Quispel, "L'Évangile selon Thomas et le Diatessaron"; *Makarius, das Thomasevangelium und das Lied von der Perle*; idem, "Some Remarks on the Gospel of Thomas"; *Tatian and the Gospel of Thomas: Studies in the History of the Western Diatessaron.*

10. Cf., e.g., A. F. J. Klijn, "Christianity in Edessa and the Gospel of Thomas," *NovT* 14 (1972): 70–77.

11. Grenfell and Hunt projected a date of 140 CE as the latest possible date for the composition of P. Oxy. 1. However, they went so far as to argue that the manuscript "might go back to the first century." See Grenfell and Hunt, *Logia Iesou*, 16.

12. In one place Perrin quips that *Thomas* is typically dated to 140 CE, "largely in unreflective dependence upon the opinion of the Oxyrhynchus discoverers, Grenfell and Hunt" ("Recent Trends in Gospel of Thomas Research (1991–2006): Part I, The Historical Jesus and the Synoptic Gospels," *CBR* 5 [2007]: 184). In his book *Thomas and Tatian* he writes, "One wonders whether 140 CE has commended itself as the

opinio communis simply because most scholars have not bothered to probe the issue" (p. 6).

13. Nicholas Perrin, *Thomas and Tatian: The Relationship between the Gospel of Thomas and the Diatessaron* (Atlanta: Society of Biblical Literature, 2002).

14. Nicholas Perrin, *Thomas: The Other Gospel* (Louisville: Westminster John Knox, 2007).

15. Ibid., 75.

16. Perrin's discussion focuses mainly on Patterson's *The Gospel of Thomas and Jesus.* See Perrin, *Thomas: The Other Gospel,* 19–36.

17. The phrase *logoi sophon* was coined by James M. Robinson in his seminal article, "LOGOI SOPHON: On the Gattung of Q," in James M. Robinson and Helmut Koester, *Trajectories Through Early Christianity* (Philadelphia: Fortress, 1971).

18. Perrin, *Thomas: The Other Gospel,* 75.

19. Perrin discusses Pagels's article, "Exegesis of Genesis 1 in the Gospels of Thomas and John," 477–96, and her book *Beyond Belief: The Secret Gospel of Thomas* (New York: Random House, 2003). See Perrin, *Thomas: The Other Gospel,* 37–51.

20. *Thomas: The Other Gospel,* 75.

21. Specifically, April D. DeConick, *Recovering the Original Gospel of Thomas: A History of the Gospel and Its Growth,* JSNTSup 286 (London: T & T Clark, 2005).

22. Ibid., 57–69.

23. Ibid., 75.

24. Perrin, "Thomas: The Fifth Gospel?" 79 (emphasis in original).

25. Ibid., 80.

26. See Enno Edzard Popkes, *Das Menschenbild des Thomasevangeliums: Untersuchungen zu seiner religionsgeschichtlichen und chronologischen Einordnung,* WUNT 206 (Tübingen: Mohr Siebeck, 2007).

27. Cf., e.g., Helmut Koester, "ΓΝΩΜΑΙ ΔΙΑΦΟΡΟΙ: The Origin and Nature of Diversification in the History of Early Christianity," *HTR* 58 (1965): 279–318; and "Apocryphal and Canonical Gospels," *HTR* 73 (1980): 105–30.

28. In a lengthy section of the book Koester discusses *Thomas*'s background, structure, and its relationship to Q and all four canonical Gospels. See pp. 75–128.

29. Ibid., 85–86.

30. It is helpful to remind the reader that Q is a hypothetical scholarly construct. A great deal of scholarship relies heavily upon the notion of Q even though we have no certain basis upon which to posit its existence. Some recent scholars have advocated dispensing with Q altogether. See, e.g., Mark Goodacre, *The Case Against Q: Studies in Markan Priority and the Synoptic Problem* (Harrisburg, PA: Trinity Press International, 2002); idem, "Fatigue in the Synoptics," *NTS* 44 (1998): 45–58; idem, "A Monopoly on Marcan Priority? Fallacies at the Heart of Q," *SBLSP* 39 (2000): 538–622.

31. Patterson, *The Gospel of Thomas and Jesus*, 17–93.

32. Ibid., 116.

33. Ibid., 116 (italics in original).

34. Both the Gospel of Mark and the Gospel of John present the disciples as failing to understand properly both Jesus' message and mission. Patterson's suggestion does not properly account for the fact that Mark is earlier than Matthew and has a much different presentation of "apostolic authority."

35. Patterson, *The Gospel of Thomas and Jesus*, 17.

36. Ibid., 120.

37. Davies, *The Gospel of Thomas and Christian Wisdom*, 3.

38. Stevan Davies, "The Christology and Protology of the Gospel of Thomas," *JBL* 111 (1992): 663 (emphasis added).

39. See Stevan Davies, "Mark's Use of the Gospel of Thomas," *Neot* 30 (1996): 307–34, and a follow-up article (coauthored with Kevin Johnson), "Mark's Use of the Gospel of Thomas, Part Two" *Neot* 31 (1997): 233–61.

40. Davies, "Mark's Use of the Gospel of Thomas," 308. My abbreviated citation does not represent a full quotation. Each point has been shortened for the sake of brevity.

41. Davies and Johnson, "Mark's Use of the Gospel of Thomas: Part Two," 259.

42. Davies, *The Gospel of Thomas and Christian Wisdom*, 17.

43. Most of the articles that follow consider one or more logia in *Thomas* with a view to assessing its antiquity vis-à-vis the canonical Gospels and, in some cases, the Pauline tradition. This question is, of course, intimately related to the question of *Thomas*'s relationship to the synoptics. Because of the interconnectedness of these discussions, some of the studies mentioned here will also be cited in chapter 3. A paradig-

matic example of this approach is Tjitze Baarda, "'Chose' or 'Collected': Concerning an Aramaism in Logion 8 of the Gospel of Thomas and the Question of Independence," *HTR* 84 (1991): 373–97. Baarda is convinced that there is archaic material in the *Gospel of Thomas* but argues that Logion 8—often regarded as an early and independent tradition—is likely dependent upon the logion in Matthew 13:47–48. An incomplete list of essays with similar approaches, premises, or conclusions includes (in alphabetical order): Tjitze Baarda, "Clement of Alexandria and the Parable of the Fisherman: Matthew 13, 47–48 or Independent Tradition?" in *The Synoptic Gospels: Source Criticism and the New Literary Criticism*, BETL 110, ed. Camille Focant (Louvain: Peeters, 1993), 582–98; idem, "'Vader—Zoon—Heilige Geest' Logion 44 van 'Thomas,'" *NedTT* 51 (1997): 13–30; idem, "'Blessed are the Poor...' Concerning the Provenance of Logion 54 in 'Thomas,'" *Essays in Honor of Frederick Wisse, ARC: The Journal of the Faculty of Religious Studies, McGill* 33 (2005): 32–51; Johannes B. Bauer, "Das 'Regelwort' Mk 6, 4 par und EvThom 31," *BZ* 41 (1997): 95–98; Edwin K. Broadhead, "An Authentic Saying of Jesus in the Gospel of Thomas?" *NTS* 48 (2000): 132–49; April D. DeConick, "On the Brink of the Apocalypse: A Preliminary Examination of the Earliest Speeches in the Gospel of Thomas," in *Thomasine Traditions in Antiquity: The Social and Cultural World of the Gospel of Thomas*, NHMS, eds. J. Asgeirsson, April D. DeConick, and R. Uro (Leiden: Brill, 2006), 93–118; Tom Thatcher, "Early Christianities and the Synoptic Eclipse: Problems in Situating the Gospel of Thomas," *BibInt* 7 (1999): 323–39; Risto Uro, "'Washing the Outside of the Cup': *Gos. Thom.* 89 and Synoptic Parallels," in *From Quest to Q: Festschrift James M. Robinson*, BETL 148 (Louvain: Peeters, 2000), 303–22.

44. Plisch, *The Gospel of Thomas: Original Text with Commentary*.

45. Ibid., 15–16.

46. Ibid., 16.

47. DeConick, *Recovering the Original Gospel of Thomas: A History of the Gospel and Its Growth*. Embryonic forms of the material published in this book can be found in DeConick's essays, "The Original Gospel of Thomas," *VC* 56 (2002): 167–99; and "Reading the *Gospel of Thomas* as a Repository of Early Christian Communal Memory," in *Memory, Tradition, and Text: Uses of the Past in Early Christianity*, Semeia Studies 52, eds. Alan Kirk and Tom Thatcher, (Atlanta: Society of Biblical Literature, 2005), 205–20.

48. April D. DeConick, *The Original Gospel of Thomas in Translation: With a Commentary and New English Translation of the Complete Gospel* (London: T & T Clark, 2006).

49. DeConick, *Recovering the Original Gospel of Thomas*, 153.

50. Ibid., 161.

51. DeConick has accused some reviewers of "misrepresenting" her views. However, a common complaint among reviewers has been that her methodology, assertions, and terminology are fuzzy and imprecise.

52. See especially, Popkes, *Das Menschenbild des Thomasevangeliums.*

Chapter 3: What Are They Saying About *Thomas*'s Relationship to the Canonical Gospels?

1. Gaertner, *The Theology of the Gospel According to Thomas*, 35, 42 (emphasis added).

2. In the previous chapter we discussed Stevan Davies's view that Mark depends on Thomas. However, since this view has won few advocates, we have chosen not to treat it here.

3. Wolfgang Schrage, *Das Verhältnis des Thomas-Evangeliums zur Synoptischen Tradition und zu den koptischen Evangelien-Übersetzungen. Zugleich ein Beitrag zur gnostischen Synoptikerdeutung*, BZNW 29 (Berlin: Töpelmann, 1964).

4. Some early critical responses to Schrage's work include reviews by R. McL. Wilson, (*VC* 20 [1966]: 118–124), Hans-Martin Schenke (*TLZ* 93 [1968]: 36–38), and Hans Quecke (*Mus* 78 [1965]: 234–39).

5. See Michael Fieger, *Das Thomasevangelium: Einleitung, Kommentar und Systematik*, NTAbh 22 (Münster, Aschendorff, 1991).

6. Ibid., 6.

7. See the following (in order of publication): Christopher Tuckett, "Thomas and the Synoptics," *NovT* 30 (1988): 132–57; idem, "Q and Thomas: Evidence of a Primitive 'Wisdom Gospel'? A Response to H. Koester," *ETL* 67 (1991): 346–60; idem, "Das Thomasevangelium und die synoptischen Evangelien," *BThZ* 12 (1995): 186–200; idem, "The Gospel of Thomas: Evidence for Jesus?," *NedTT* 52 (1998): 17–32.

8. See the previous note for full bibliographic information.

9. Tuckett, "Thomas and the Synoptics," 156.

10. Ibid., 156–57.

11. Tuckett, "Q and Thomas: Evidence of a Primitive 'Wisdom Gospel'?" *ETL* 67 (1991): 346–60.

12. Ibid., 349.

13. Ibid., 359.

14. Tuckett is clear about this aim. He writes, "In an earlier study I have tried to show that GTh shows dependence on Mark's gospel. In that study, and in the remarks given here, I have tried to show that GTh also shows agreement with MtR and LkR at times" ("Q and Thomas," 359).

15. Thomas Zöckler, *Jesu Lehren im Thomasevangelium*, NHMS 47 (Leiden/New York/ Cologne: Brill, 1999).

16. See the discussion in Patterson, *The Gospel of Thomas and Jesus*, 17–91.

17. Ibid., 17.

18. Ibid., 99.

19. Ibid., 16.

20. Ibid., 93.

21. Charles W. Hedrick, "An Anecdotal Argument for the Independence of the Gospel of Thomas from the Synoptic Gospels," in Hans-Gephardt Bethge, et. al. eds., *For the Children, Perfect Instruction: Studies in Honor of Hans-Martin Schenke on the Occasion of the Berliner Arbeitskreis für koptisch-gnostische Schriften's Thirtieth Year*, NHMS 54 (Leiden: Brill, 2002), 114.

22. Ibid., 114.

23. Gregory J. Riley, "Influence of Thomas Christianity on Luke 12:14 and 5:39," *HTR* 88 (1995): 229–35.

24. Ibid., 231.

25. Ibid., 235.

26. The most extreme example of such an investigation in Riley's case is his thesis about the Fourth Gospel's supposed polemic against Thomas Christianity. This is covered in the following section on *Thomas and the Gospel of John.*

27. Cf. Steven R. Johnson, "The Hidden/Revealed Saying in the Greek and Coptic Versions of Gos. Thom. 5 & 6," *NovT* 44 (2002): 176–85; idem, "The Gospel of Thomas 76.3 and Canonical Parallels: Three Segments in the Tradition History of the Saying," in John D. Turner and Anne McGuire, eds., *The Nag Hammadi Library After Fifty*

Years: Proceedings of the 1995 Society of Biblical Literature Commemoration, NHMS 44 (Leiden: Brill, 1997), 308–25.

28. Steven R. Johnson, *Seeking the Imperishable Treasure: Wealth, Wisdom, and a Jesus Saying* (Eugene, OR: Cascade, 2008).

29. In his review of Johnson's monograph, Thomas Phillips appropriately comments: "As with any investigation of this sort, the conclusions are tentative and will prove persuasive only to those who share most or all of Johnson's presumptions about the historical relationships between the various documents" (see Thomas E. Phillips's review of Steven R. Johnson, *Seeking the Imperishable Treasure: Wealth, Wisdom, and a Jesus Saying*, in *RSR* 36 [2010]: 147). I could not agree more with this assessment.

30. He writes, "Simply put, the author of Luke was a collector and adapter of sources. While Luke's primary source was Q, aspects of the Thomas version were integrated in the process of redacting Q. The Lukan focus in this operation appears to have been less a concern for correcting the interpretation of the Thomas version and more a concern for focusing the interpretation of the Q version on specific, concrete, Lukan concerns. In other words, at least in this case, the author of Luke does not appear to have had a particular bone to pick with the tradition represented by Thomas 76.3" (Johnson, "The Gospel of Thomas 76.3 and Canonical Parallels," 320–21).

31. In his book he concludes, "[C]lose and careful studies of individual sayings in Thomas—sayings that find their parallels in the canonical literature and elsewhere—must continue to be done in order to gain a more precise and detailed picture of the history and development of the Gospel of Thomas and its historical relationship to sayings traditions represented by other texts" (Johnson, *Seeking the Imperishable Treasure*, 152).

32. Simon Gathercole, "Luke in the *Gospel of Thomas*," *NTS* 57 (2011): 114–44.

33. Ibid., 143.

34. Ibid. (italics in original).

35. Raymond E. Brown, "The *Gospel of Thomas* and St. John's Gospel," *NTS* 9 (1962): 155–77.

36. Ibid., 177.

37. M. Marcovich, "Textual Criticism on the *Gospel of Thomas*." *JTS* 20 (1969): 53–74.

38. Jesse Sell, "Johannine Traditions in Logion 61 of the *Gospel of Thomas*," *PRSt* 7 (1980): 24–37; idem, "A Study of the Self-Predication

Statements Attributed to 'Jesus Christ' in the Naga-Hammadi Coptic 'Gnostic' Corpus," (Ph.D. diss., Duke University, 1976). The eight sayings identified by Sell are the *Gospel of Thomas* prologue, 8, 13, 28, 38, 43, 91, and 92.

39. Sell, "Johannine Traditions," 24.

40. Gregory J. Riley, *Resurrection Reconsidered: John and Thomas in Controversy* (Minneapolis: Fortress, 1995).

41. Riley is also concerned, but only peripherally, with the *Book of Thomas* and the *Acts of Thomas*—other literature arising from the Thomas tradition within early Christianity.

42. Riley, *Resurrection Reconsidered*, 177.

43. Ibid., 74–82, esp. 78.

44. Parallel sayings are found six different places in the canonical literature: Mark 14:58; 15:29; Matt 26:61; 27:40; John 2:19; and Acts 6:14.

45. Riley, *Resurrection Reconsidered*, 148–49.

46. See her discussion in "'Blessed Are Those Who Have Not Seen' (Jn 20:29): Johannine Dramatization of an Early Christian Discourse," in John D. Turner and Anne McGuire, eds., *The Nag Hammadi Library after Fifty Years. Proceedings of the 1995 Society of Biblical Literature Commemoration*, NHMS 44 (Leiden: Brill, 1997) 381–98. See also DeConick's revised dissertation, *Seek to See Him: Ascent and Vision Mysticism in the Gospel of Thomas*, VCSup 33 (Leiden: Brill, 1996).

47. DeConick, "John Rivals Thomas: From Community Conflict to Gospel Narrative," in Tom Thatcher and Robert Fortna, eds., *Jesus in the Johannine Tradition: New Directions* (Louisville: Westminster John Knox, 2001) 303–11.

48. Ibid., 307.

49. See April D. DeConick, *Voices of the Mystics: Early Christian Discourse in the Gospels of John and Thomas and Other Ancient Christian Literature*, JSNTSup 157 (Sheffield: Sheffield Academic Press, 2001).

50. DeConick ("Blessed Are Those Who Have Not Seen," 391) writes: "The main issue in all three of these [*Thomas*] episodes [in the Fourth Gospel] is one of identity, not Jesus' corporeality as some have suggested." The accompanying footnote references Riley's *Resurrection Reconsidered* as the most recent work offering this purportedly mistaken suggestion.

51. DeConick distinguishes between the wider "religio-social horizon," or the specific religious community John is concerned to dis-

pute, and the "discursive field," or the particular point of conflict between the two groups ("Blessed Are Those Who Have Not Seen," 383).

52. DeConick, "John Rivals Thomas," 305.

53. DeConick, "Blessed Are Those Who Have Not Seen," 382.

54. Ibid., 390–91 (emphasis added).

55. Elaine Pagels, *The Gnostic Gospels* (New York: Random House, 1979).

56. Pagels, "Exegesis of Genesis 1 in the Gospels of Thomas and John," *JBL* 118 (1999): 477–96.

57. Ibid., 479.

58. Ibid., 481.

59. Ibid., 481.

60. She writes, "Let us begin from the opening of Thomas's Gospel, adopting the hypothesis that the sayings are not randomly arranged, but carefully ordered to lead one through a process of seeing and finding 'the interpretation of these sayings' (log. 1). This is not to suggest, however, that the author follows an obvious or syllogistic rationale" (ibid., 481).

61. Pagels's basis for this assumption is found in the conclusions offered by J. Z. Smith, "The Garments of Shame," *HR* 5 (1966): 217–38.

62. Pagels, "Exegesis of Genesis 1," 488.

63. Elaine Pagels, *Beyond Belief: The Secret Gospel of Thomas* (San Francisco: HarperCollins, 2003).

64. Ibid., 30–73.

65. Ibid., 72.

66. Material from the articles "John and Thomas in Conflict?" (originally published in *The Nag Hammadi Library After Fifty Years*); "The Beloved Disciple in John: Ideal Figure in an Early Christian Controversy?" (originally published in *Fair Play: Diversity and Conflicts in Early Christianity* [Leiden: Brill, 2001]); "Thomas's I-Sayings and the Gospel of John"; and "Thomas and the Beloved Disciple" (both published in Risto Uro, ed., *Thomas at the Crossroads: Essays on the Gospel of Thomas*, Studies of the New Testament and Its World [Edinburgh: T & T Clark, 1998]) was reworked and constitutes the substantive discussion of the book.

67. Ismo Dunderberg, *The Beloved Disciple in Conflict? Revisiting the Gospels of John and Thomas* (Oxford: Oxford University Press, 2006).

68. Ibid., 200.

69. Ibid., 200.

70. See Christopher W. Skinner, *John and Thomas: Gospels in Conflict? Johannine Characterization and the Thomas Question*, PTMS 115 (Eugene, OR: Pickwick, 2009), esp. 19–41.

71. Ibid., 232.

72. See Nicholas Perrin, *Thomas and Tatian: The Relationship between the Gospel of Thomas and the Diatessaron* (Atlanta: Society of Biblical Literature, 2002); idem, "Thomas: The Fifth Gospel?" *JETS* 49 (2006): 67–80; idem, *Thomas: The Other Gospel* (Louisville: Westminster John Knox, 2007).

73. Quispel, *Tatian and the Gospel of Thomas*.

74. Perrin, *Thomas and Tatian*, 50.

75. Ibid., 156.

76. Perrin, "Thomas: The Fifth Gospel?" 79.

77. Critical reviews of Perrin's thesis can be found in *JBL* 122 (2003): 387–91; *ExpTim* 114 (2003): 310–13; and *VC* 58 (2004): 205–6. See also, Peter J. Williams, "Alleged Aramaic Catchwords in the Gospel of Thomas," *VC* 63 (2009): 71–82.

78. Peter Nagel, "Erwägungen zum Thomas-Evangelium," in F. Altheim and R. Stiehl, eds., *Die Araber in der alten Welt*, Volume V, Part 2 (Berlin: Walter de Gruyter, 1969), 368–92.

79. Ibid., 368–69.

80. Ibid., 371.

81. Stephen J. Patterson, "Paul and the Jesus Tradition: It Is Time for Another Look," *HTR* 84 (1991): 36–7 (emphasis added).

82. Christopher Tuckett, "Paul and Jesus Tradition: The Evidence of 1 Corinthians 2:9 and Gospel of Thomas 17," in J. Andreas Lowe, T. J. Burke, and J. K. Elliott, eds., *Paul and the Corinthians: Studies on a Community in Conflict: Essays in Honour of Margaret Thrall*, NovTSup 109 (Leiden Brill, 2003), 55–73.

83. Ibid., 73.

84. Simon Gathercole, "The Influence of Paul on the Gospel of Thomas," in Jorg Frey, E. E. Popkes, and Jens Schroter, eds., *Das Thomas-evangelium: Entstehung—Rezeption—Theologie*, BZNW 157 (Berlin: Walter de Gruyter, 2008) 72–94.

85. Ibid., 84.

86. Christopher W. Skinner, "The *Gospel of Thomas's* Rejection of Paul's Theological Ideas," in Michael F. Bird and Joel Willitts, eds., *Paul*

and the Gospels: Christologies, Conflicts, and Convergences, LNTS (London: T&T Clark, 2011), 220–41.

87. Rom 10:5–8 & *Gos. Thom.* 3; 1 Cor 2:9 & *Gos. Thom.* 17; 2 Cor 4:7 & *Gos. Thom.* 29; Rom 2:25–29 & *Gos. Thom.* 53; 2 Cor 4:16–18 & *Gos. Thom.* 70; and Rom 7:24 & *Gos. Thom.* 87.

88. Skinner, "The *Gospel of Thomas*'s Rejection of Paul's Theological Ideas," 238.

89. Joshua W. Jipp, "Death and the Human Predicament, Salvation as Transformation, and Bodily Practices in 1 Corinthians and the *Gospel of Thomas*," in Michael F. Bird and Joel Willitts, eds., *Paul and the Gospels: Christologies, Conflicts, and Convergences*, LNTS (London: T&T Clark, 2011), 242–66.

90. Ibid., 266.

Chapter 4: What Are They Saying About *Thomas*'s Theological Outlook?

1. Boudewijn Dehandschutter, "Recent Research on the Gospel of Thomas," in F. van Segbroeck, ed., *Four Gospels*, BETL 100 (Louvain: Peeters, 1992), 3:2262.

2. Among others, see Grant and Freedman, *The Secret Sayings of Jesus*; Wilson, *Studies in the Gospel of Thomas*; Gartner, *The Theology of the Gospel According to Thomas*; Kasser, *L'Évangile Selon Thomas: Présentation et commentaire théologique*; and Leipoldt, *Das Evangelium nach Thomas*.

3. For his part, Gilles Quispel regarded *Thomas* as a Jewish-Christian gospel that was based on a gospel that is now lost. The hypothetical "lost gospel" may have had some connection to the *Gospel of the Nazoreans* and/or the *Gospel of the Hebrews*. Since Quispel was one of the first scholars to examine *Thomas* thoroughly, his view should properly be considered the first scholarly opinion on *Thomas*'s theological outlook. However, his viewpoint was quickly overtaken by the rampant speculation about *Thomas*'s Gnostic origins. See the pertinent sections in the following (in chronological order): "The Gospel of Thomas and the New Testament"; "Some Remarks on the Gospel of Thomas," *NTS* 5 (1958/1959): 276–90; "L'Évangile selon Thomas et les Clementines," *VC* 12 (1958): 181–96; "L'Évangile selon Thomas et le Diatessaron," *VC* 13

(1959): 87–117; "The 'Gospel of Thomas' and the 'Gospel of the Hebrews,'" *NTS* 12 (1966): 371–82.

4. As already stated, Helmut Koester regarded *Thomas* as an example of wisdom literature. His views and publications remain a fixture in discussions of *Thomas*'s theological outlook. For a list of his important publications on this issue, see note 9 in chapter 1.

5. This point is made by a number of scholars, most recently by Petr Pokorny, *A Commentary on the Gospel of Thomas: From Interpretations to the Interpreted,* Jewish and Christian Texts in Contexts and Related Studies 5 (London/New York: T & T Clark, 2009).

6. Stevan Davies, "Thomas: The Fourth Synoptic Gospel," *BA* 46 (1983): 7.

7. On this topic, see Michael Williams, *Rethinking "Gnosticism": An Argument for Dismantling a Dubious Category* (Princeton: Princeton University Press, 1996).

8. See, principally, Lucien Cerfaux and Gérard Garitte, "Les paraboles du Royaume dans L'Évangile de Thomas," *Mus* 70 (1957): 307–27.

9. See, among others, William Schoedel, "Naassene Themes in the Coptic Gospel of Thomas," *VC* 14 (1960): 225–34.

10. On this progression of thought, see the very helpful overview provided in April D. DeConick, "The Gospel of Thomas," *ExpTim* 118 (2007): 471–72.

11. Michael Fieger, *Das Thomasevangelium: Einleitung, Kommentar und Systematik,* NTAbh 22 (Münster, Aschendorff, 1991).

12. Stephen J. Patterson, review of Michael Fieger, *Das Thomasevangelium: Einleitung, Kommentar und Systematik,* *JBL* 111 (1992): 361–63.

13. Enno Edzard Popkes, *Das Menschenbild des Thomasevangeliums: Untersuchungen zu seiner religionsgeschichtlichen und chronologischen Einordnung,* WUNT 206 (Tübingen: Mohr Siebeck, 2007).

14. See, e.g., *The Gnostic Bible: Revised and Expanded Edition,* coedited with Willis Barnstone (Boston & London: New Seeds: 2009); *The Gnostic Discoveries: The Impact of the Nag Hammadi Library* (San Francisco: HarperOne, 2006); *The Gnostic Gospels of Jesus: The Definitive Collection of Mystical Gospels and Secret Books about Jesus of Nazareth* (San Francisco: HarperOne, 2005).

15. Meyer, *The Gospel of Thomas.*

16. Meyer, *The Gnostic Gospels of Jesus*, 3.

17. William Arnal, "The Rhetoric of Marginality: Apocalypticism, Gnosticism, and Sayings Gospels," *HTR* 88 (1995): 478.

18. Antti Marjanen, "Is *Thomas* a Gnostic Gospel?," in Risto Uro, ed. *Thomas at the Crossroads*, 107–39.

19. Ibid., 138.

20. "Are *Thomas*'s and thus also John's views of the world then Gnostic? If a Gnostic writing has to distinguish between a good, eternal God and a perishable, malevolent creator, as is done in the *Gospel of Philip* or the *Apocryphon of John*, one has to answer no. If the fact that a writing regards the world as evil and as being in opposition to the divine realm makes its conception of the world Gnostic, one can answer yes" (ibid., 139).

21. See the helpful discussion in R. McL. Wilson, "The Gospel of Thomas Reconsidered," in Cäcilia Fluck, Lucia Langener, Siegfried Richter, Sofia Schaten, and Gregor Wurst, eds., *Divitiae Aegypti Koptologische und verwandte Studien zu Ehren von Martin Krause* (Wiesbaden: Dr. Ludwig Reichert Verlag, 1995), 331–33.

22. In 1971, Koester and James M. Robinson published an important book entitled *Trajectories through Early Christianity* (Philadelphia: Fortress, 1971). The book was a compilation of four previously published articles (two by each author) along with four new essays (also two by each author). The volume was driven by the assumption that historical discoveries and developments in our understanding of NT backgrounds render terms like "heresy" and "orthodoxy" inadequate. Rather, an appreciation for the intricate web of continuity and diversity among the early "Christian" communities opens new doors of historical investigation that shed light on the complexity of early Christianity and its many expressions—both kerygmatic and literary.

23. Patterson, *The Gospel of Thomas and Jesus*, 218–19.

24. Plisch, *The Gospel of Thomas*, 33.

25. Hans-Martin Schenke, "Die Tendenz der Weisheit zur Gnosis," in Barbara Aland, ed., *Gnosis: Festschrift für Hans Jonas* (Göttingen: Vandenhoeck und Ruprecht, 1978), 351–72.

26. Alexei Siverstev, "The *Gospel of Thomas* and Early Stages in the Development of the Christian Wisdom Literature," *JECS* 8 (2000): 319–40.

27. Ibid., 340.

28. See, e.g., Richard Valantasis, "Is the Gospel of Thomas Ascetical? Revisiting an Old Problem with a New Theory," *JECS* 7 (1999): 55–81.

29. Ibid., 22.

30. Ibid., 59.

31. See the pertinent discussion in Valantasis, "Is the Gospel of Thomas Ascetical?," 57–58.

32. Ibid., 61.

33. Ibid., 61.

34. Valantasis, *The Gospel of Thomas*, 22.

35. Risto Uro, "Is *Thomas* an Encratite Gospel?," in Risto Uro, ed. *Thomas at the Crossroads: Essays on the Gospel of Thomas*, Studies of the New Testament and Its World (Edinburgh: T & T Clark, 1998), 140–62.

36. This discussion can be found in his book, *Thomas: Seeking the Historical Context of the Gospel of Thomas* (London: T & T Clark, 2003).

37. See, in chronological order, *Seek to See Him: Ascent and Vision Mysticism in the Gospel of Thomas*, VCSup 33 (Leiden: Brill, 1996); *Voices of the Mystics: Early Christian Discourse in the Gospels of John and Thomas and Other Ancient Christian Literature* (London: T & T Clark, 2001); *Recovering the Original Gospel of Thomas* (2005); *The Original Gospel of Thomas in Translation* (2006). See also, Jon Ma. Asgeirsson, April D. DeConick and Risto Uro, eds., *Thomasine Traditions in Antiquity: The Social and Cultural World of the Gospel of Thomas*, NHMS 59 (Leiden: Brill, 2006).

38. See, in chronological order, "The Yoke Saying in the Gospel of Thomas 90," *VC* 44 (1990): 280–94; (coauthored with Jarl Fossum), "Stripped before God: A New Interpretation of Logion 37 in the Gospel of Thomas," *VC* 45 (1991): 123–50; "The Original Gospel of Thomas," *VC* 56 (2002): 167–99; "Reading the Gospel of Thomas as a Repository of Early Christian Communal Memory" in Alan Kirk and Tom Thatcher, eds., *Memory, Tradition, and Text: Uses of the Past in Early Christianity*, SemeiaSt 52 (Atlanta: Society of Biblical Literature, 2005), 207–220; "Corrections to the Critical Reading of the Gospel of Thomas" *VC* 60 (2006): 201–208; "The Gospel of Thomas," *ExpTim* 118 (2007): 469–79; "Mysticism in the Gospel of Thomas," in Jorg Frey, E. E. Popkes, and Jens Schroter, eds., *Das Thomasevangelium: Entstehung—Rezeption—Theologie*, BZNW 157 (Berlin: Walter de Gruyter, 2008), 206–21; "What's Up with the Gospel of Thomas?" *BAR* 36 (2010): 28, 85.

39. This understanding of *Thomas*'s theological outlook plays an important role in her books, *Seek to See Him* (1996), and *Voices of the Mystics* (2001).

40. DeConick, "The Gospel of Thomas," 478–79 (emphasis added).

41. April D. DeConick, "Mysticism and the *Gospel of Thomas*," in *Das Thomasevangelium: Entstehung, Rezeption, Theologie*, BZNW 157 (Berlin & New York: Walter de Gruyter, 2008), 221.

42. April D. DeConick, *Seek to See Him: Ascent and Vision Mysticism in the Gospel of Thomas*, VCSup 33 (Leiden: Brill, 1996).

43. Ibid., 38.

44. April D. DeConick, *Voices of the Mystics: Early Christian Discourse in the Gospels of John and Thomas and Other Ancient Christian Literature*, JSNTSup 157 (Sheffield: Sheffield Academic Press, 2001).

45. DeConick, "The Gospel of Thomas," 479.

46. Howard M. Jackson, *The Lion Becomes Man: The Gnostic Leontomorphic Creator and the Platonic Tradition*, SBLDS 81 (Atlanta: Scholars Press, 1985).

47. Translation is the author's own.

48. Jackson, *The Lion Becomes Man*, 212.

49. Andrew Crislip has argued that, while Jackson's study is learned and helpful in a number of respects, *Gos. Thom.* 7 is probably not rooted in Platonism but in an early Christian discourse concerning the resurrection. See his study, "Lion and Human in *Gospel of Thomas* Logion 7," *JBL* 126 (2007): 595–613.

50. John M. Dillon, "Middle Platonism," in Robert Audi, ed., *The Cambridge Dictionary of Philosophy* (Cambridge: Cambridge University Press, 1995), 492–93.

51. Stephen J. Patterson, "Understanding the *Gospel of Thomas* Today," in Stephen J. Patterson, James M. Robinson, and Hans-Gebhard Bethge, *The Fifth Gospel: The Gospel of Thomas Comes of Age* (Harrisburg, PA: Trinity Press International, 1998), 33–75.

52. Ibid., 59 (italics added).

53. Stephen J. Patterson, "Jesus Meets Plato: The Theology of the Gospel of Thomas and Middle Platonism," in *Das Thomasevangelium: Entstehung, Rezeption, Theologie*, BZNW 157 (Berlin & New York: Walter de Gruyter, 2008), 181–205.

54. Ibid., 205.

Chapter 5: The *Gospel of Thomas* and the Historical Jesus

1. For different views on *Thomas*'s role in historical Jesus scholarship, see the pertinent sections in Perrin, "Recent Trends," 185–91; Stephen J. Patterson, "The Gospel of Thomas and Historical Jesus Research," in Louis Painchaud and Paul-Hubert Poirier, eds., *Coptica— gnostica—manichaica: mélanges offerts à Wolf-Peter Funk*, Bibliothèque copte de Nag Hammadi Études 7 (Quebec: Les Presses de l'Université Laval; Paris: Éditions Peeters, 2006), 663–84; and Charles Hedrick, ed., "The Historical Jesus and the Rejected Gospels," *Semeia* 44 (1988): 9–140.

2. John P. Meier, *A Marginal Jew: Rethinking the Historical Jesus. Volume I: The Roots of the Problem and Person*, ABRL (New York: Doubleday, 1991). Subsequent volumes were released under the same title with the following subtitles: *Volume II: Mentor, Message, and Miracles*, ABRL (New York: Doubleday, 1994); *Volume III: Companions and Competitors*, ABRL (New York: Doubleday, 2001); and *Volume IV: Law and Love*, Anchor Yale Bible Reference Library (New Haven: Yale University Press, 2009).

3. Robert W. Funk, Roy W. Hoover, and the Jesus Seminar, eds. *The Five Gospels: The Search for the Authentic Words of Jesus* (San Francisco: Harper San Francisco, 1993).

4. John Dominic Crossan, *The Historical Jesus: The Life of a Mediterranean Jewish Peasant* (San Francisco: HarperCollins, 1991).

5. Meier, *A Marginal Jew*, 1:124–39.

6. Ibid., 126.

7. Ibid., 126.

8. He writes, "However, this 2d-century date and the Gnostic character of the final document do not answer the question of whether some early source of authentic sayings of Jesus, perhaps even earlier and more original than what we find in the Synoptics, might be preserved in the *Gospel of Thomas*. The debate on this point has been lively and varied, and it is not likely to come to rest soon" (ibid., 127).

9. The following five points represent a summarized form of arguments that appear throughout pp. 130–39.

10. Ibid., 130.

11. Ibid., 139.

12. Ibid., 139.

13. Toward the end of his argument he writes: "Contrary to some scholars, I do not think that the rabbinic material, the *agrapha*, the apocryphal gospels, and the Nag Hammadi codices (in particular the *Gospel of Thomas*) offer us reliable new information or authentic sayings that are independent of the NT. What we see in these later documents is rather the reaction to or reworking of NT writings by Jewish rabbis engaged in polemics, imaginative Christians reflecting popular piety and legend, and Gnostic Christians developing a mystic speculative system" (ibid., 140).

14. The list of detractors is long and includes, among others, D. A. Carson, "Five Gospels, No Christ," *Christianity Today* (April 1994): 30–33; Robert Yarbrough, "The Gospel According to the Jesus Seminar," *Presb* 20 (1994): 8–20; Robert L. Thomas, "Evangelical Responses to the Jesus Seminar," *MSJ* 7 (1996): 75–105; Ben Witherington, *The Jesus Quest: The Third Search for the Jew of Nazareth,* 2d ed. (Downers Grove, IL: InterVarsity, 1997); Richard B. Hays, "The Corrected Jesus," *First Things* 43 (1994): 43–48; Jeffrey A. Gibbs, "The Search for the Idiosyncratic Jesus: A Critique of the Jesus Seminar's *The Five Gospels*," *Concordia Journal* (October 1994): 368–84; and Luke Timothy Johnson, *The Real Jesus: The Misguided Quest for the Historical Jesus and the Truth of the Traditional Gospels* (San Francisco: HarperCollins, 1996). See also the very helpful overview of the Jesus Seminar and its critics found in David B. Gowler, *What Are They Saying About the Historical Jesus?* (Mahwah, NJ: Paulist, 2007), 31–57.

15. Several critics have argued that the Jesus Seminar's "aggressive media campaign" has made it nearly impossible for the public to ignore them. The most sustained treatment of this issue has been set forth in Johnson, *The Real Jesus,* 1–27.

16. Funk and Hoover, *The Five Gospels,* 36.

17. Robert J. Miller, "The Jesus Seminar and the Search for the Words of Jesus," *LTQ* 31 (1996): 110.

18. Three sayings are coded red: *Gos. Thom.* 20, 54, and 100. Portions of 33 sayings are coded in pink: 2, 5, 6, 9, 10, 14, 26, 31, 32, 33, 35, 36, 39, 41, 45, 47, 62, 63, 64, 65, 69, 76, 78, 86, 89, 92, 94, 95, 96, 97, 98, 109, and 113.

19. Miller, "The Jesus Seminar," 111.

20. Charles L. Quarles, "The Use of the *Gospel of Thomas* in the Research on the Historical Jesus of John Dominic Crossan," *CBQ* 69 (2007): 517.

21. Among others, see (in chronological order) John Dominic Crossan, *In Parables: The Challenge of the Historical Jesus* (Sonoma, CA: Polebridge, 1992); *Jesus: A Revolutionary Biography* (San Francisco: HarperSanFrancisco: 1994); *The Essential Jesus: Original Sayings and Earliest Images* (San Francisco: HarperSanFrancisco, 1994); *Who Killed Jesus? Exposing the Roots of Anti-Semitism in the Gospel Story of the Death of Jesus* (San Francisco: HarperOne, 1996); *Who Is Jesus? Answers to Your Questions About the Historical Jesus* (Louisville: Westminster John Knox, 1999) (with Richard C. Watts); *The Birth of Christianity: Discovering What Happened in the Years Immediately After the Execution of Jesus* (San Francisco: HarperOne, 1999); *Excavating Jesus: Beneath the Stones, Behind the Texts* (San Francisco: HarperCollins, 2002) (with Jonathan L. Reed); and *God and Empire: Jesus Against Rome, Then and Now* (San Francisco: HarperOne, 2007).

22. Crossan, *The Historical Jesus*, xiii–xxvi.

23. See Helmut Koester, *Introduction to the New Testament*, 2 vols., Hermeneia Foundation and Facets (Philadelphia: Fortress, 1982), 2:121–22.

24. See Davies, *The Gospel of Thomas and Christian Wisdom*.

25. See John S. Kloppenborg, *The Formation of Q: Trajectories in Ancient Wisdom Collections*, SAC (Philadelphia: Fortress, 1987).

26. Crossan, *The Historical Jesus*, 230 (emphasis added).

27. See, in particular, the very helpful critiques most recently leveled against Crossan's approach in Quarles, "The Use of the *Gospel of Thomas* in the Research on the Historical Jesus of John Dominic Crossan," 517–36.

SELECT BIBLIOGRAPHY

The list of resources below is incomplete and is intended to provide interested readers with avenues for further research. The works are categorized as follows:

* Accessible to the nonspecialist
** Written on an academic level but accessible to an educated nonspecialist
*** Intended for those with background knowledge of early Christian literature and the requisite research languages

I. English Translations

Guillamont, Antoine, Henri-Charles Puech, Gilles Quispel, and Y. 'Abd al Masih. *The Gospel According to Thomas: Coptic Text Established and Translated*. Leiden: Brill, 1959.

Layton, Bentley. *The Gnostic Scriptures: A New Translation with Annotations and Introductions*. ABRL. New Haven: Yale University Press, 1995, 376–99.

Meyer, Marvin. *The Gnostic Gospels of Jesus: The Definitive Collection of Mystical Gospels and Secret Books about Jesus of Nazareth*. San Francisco: HarperOne, 2005, 7–30.

————, trans. *The Nag Hammadi Scriptures: The International Edition*. *Gospel of Thomas*. San Francisco: HarperOne, 2007, 133–56.

Robinson, James M., ed. *The Nag Hammadi Library in English*. *Gospel of Thomas*. Translated by Helmut Koester and Thomas O. Lambdin. San Francisco: HarperOne, 1990, 124–38.

Schneemelcher, Wilhelm, ed. *New Testament Apocrypha: Volume 1. Gospels and Related Writings. Gospel of Thomas.* Translated by Beate Blatz. Louisville: Westminster John Knox, 1991, 110–33.

II. *Thomas* Within Early Christianity

Asgeirsson, Jon Ma., April D. DeConick, and Risto Uro. *Thomasine Traditions in Antiquity: The Social and Cultural World of the Gospel of Thomas.* NHMS 59. Leiden: Brill, 2006.***

Davies, Stevan. *The Gospel of Thomas and Christian Wisdom.* 2nd ed. Dublin: Bardic Press, 2005.**

DeConick, April D. *Recovering the Original Gospel of Thomas: A History of the Gospel and Its Growth.* LNTS 286. Edinburgh: T & T Clark, 2005.***

Patterson, Stephen J. *The Gospel of Thomas and Jesus.* Sonoma, CA: Polebridge Press, 1992.***

Patterson, Stephen J., James M. Robinson, and Hans-Gebhard Bethge. *The Fifth Gospel: The Gospel of Thomas Comes of Age.* Harrisburg, PA: Trinity Press International, 1998.*

Perrin, Nicholas. *Thomas: The Other Gospel.* Louisville: Westminster John Knox, 2007.**

Uro, Risto. *Thomas at the Crossroads: Essays on the Gospel of Thomas.* Studies of the New Testament and Its World. Edinburgh: T & T Clark, 1998.**

———. *Thomas: Seeking the Historical Context of the Gospel of Thomas.* London: T & T Clark, 2003.**

III. Commentaries

A. *Older Commentaries*

Gaertner, Bertil. *The Theology of the Gospel According to Thomas.* Translated by Eric J. Sharpe. New York: Harper, 1961.**

Grant, Robert M., and David Noel Freedman. *The Secret Sayings of Jesus.* Garden City, NY: Doubleday, 1960.**

Kasser, Rodolphe. *L'Évangile Selon Thomas: Présentation et commentaire théologique.* Biliothèque Theologique. Neuchatel: Delachaux et Niestlé, 1961.***

Leipoldt, Johannes. *Das Evangelium nach Thomas.* Berlin: Akademie–Verlag, 1967.***

Wilson, R. McL. *Studies in the Gospel of Thomas.* London: Mobray, 1960.**

B. Recent Commentaries

Davies, Stevan. *The Gospel of Thomas: Annotated and Explained.* Woodstock, VT: Skylight Paths Publishing, 2002.*

DeConick, April D. *The Original Gospel of Thomas in Translation: With a Commentary and New English Translation of the Complete Gospel.* LNTS 287. Edinburgh: T & T Clark, 2007.***

Fieger, Michael. *Das Thomasevangelium: Einleitung, Kommentar und Systematik.* NTAbh 22. Münster: Aschendorff, 1991.***

Hedrick, Charles W. *Unlocking the Secrets of the Gospel according to Thomas: A Radical Faith for a New Age.* Eugene, OR: Cascade, 2010.*

Meyer, Marvin. *The Gospel of Thomas: The Hidden Sayings of Jesus.* San Francisco: HarperSanFrancisco, 1992.*

Plisch, Uwe-Karsten. *The Gospel of Thomas: Original Text with Commentary.* Peabody, MA: Hendrickson, 2009.***

Pokorny, Petr. *A Commentary on the Gospel of Thomas: From Interpretations to the Interpreted.* Jewish and Christian Texts in Contexts and Related Studies 5. London/New York: T & T Clark, 2009.***

Valantasis, Richard. *The Gospel of Thomas.* New Testament Readings. New York: Routledge, 1997.**

IV. *Thomas* and Early Christian Literature

DeConick, April D. *Voices of the Mystics: Early Christian Discourse in the Gospels of John and Thomas and Other Ancient Christian Literature.* JSNTSup 157. Sheffield: Sheffield Academic Press, 2001.***

Dunderberg, Ismo. *The Beloved Disciple in Conflict? Revisiting the Gospels of John and Thomas.* Oxford: Oxford University Press, 2006.**

Pagels, Elaine. *Beyond Belief: The Secret Gospel of Thomas.* San Francisco: HarperCollins, 2003.*

Perrin, Nicholas. *Thomas and Tatian: The Relationship Between the Gospel of Thomas and the Diatessaron.* AcBib 5. Atlanta: Society of Biblical Literature, 2003.***

Quispel, Gilles. *Tatian and the Gospel of Thomas: Studies in the History of the Western Diatessaron.* Leiden: Brill, 1975.***

Riley, Gregory J. *Resurrection Reconsidered: John and Thomas in Controversy.* Minneapolis: Fortress, 1995.**

Skinner, Christopher W. *John and Thomas: Gospels in Conflict? Johannine Characterization and the Thomas Question.* PTMS 115. Eugene, OR: Pickwick, 2009.***

V. Surveys of *Thomas* Research

Dehandschutter, B. "Recent Research on the *Gospel of Thomas*." In F. van Segbroeck, ed., *Four Gospels.* BETL 100. Louvain: Peeters, 1992, 3:2257–2262.**

Fallon, Francis T. and Ron Cameron. "The Gospel of Thomas: A *Forschungsbericht* and Analysis." *ANRW* 2:25.6 (1988): 4195–4251.**

Patterson, Stephen J. "The Gospel of Thomas and the Synoptic Tradition: A Forschungsbericht and Analysis." *FFF* 8 (1992): 45–97.**

Perrin, Nicholas. "Recent Trends in *Gospel of Thomas* Research (1991–2006): Part I, The Historical Jesus and the Synoptic Gospels." *CBR* 5 (2007): 183–206.**

Perrin, Nicholas, and Christopher W. Skinner, "Recent Trends in *Gospel of Thomas* Research (1989–2010): Part II. *CBR* (forthcoming 2012).**

VI. Important Related Reading

Bauer, Walter. *Orthodoxy and Heresy in Earliest Christianity*. Philadelphia: Fortress, 1979.**

Robinson, James M., and Helmut Koester. *Trajectories through Early Christianity*. Philadelphia: Fortress, 1971.**

Koester, Helmut. *Ancient Christian Gospels: Their History and Development*. Harrisburg, PA: Trinity Press International, 1992.**

VII. Helpful Online Resources

"Early Christian Writings" (*http://www.earlychristianwritings.com/ thomas.html*). This site contains over fifteen English translations along with a few links to the Coptic text on the Web.

"The Gnostic Society Library: Gospel of Thomas Collection" (*http:// www.gnosis.org/naghamm/nhl_thomas.htm*). This site contains translations, introductions, and links to other sites dealing with the *Gospel of Thomas*.

"The Gospel of Thomas Resource Center" (*http://gospel-thomas.net/*). Maintained by Mike Grondin, this is a helpful site for studying the *Gospel of Thomas*. The site contains introductory material, maps, background discussion, and a Coptic-English interlinear translation for the full text of the *Gospel of Thomas*.

"*Gospel of Thomas* Homepage" (*http://home.epix.net/~miser17/Thomas. html*). This site is maintained by Stevan Davies and consists of links to other sites and material helpful for studying the *Gospel of Thomas* as well as other ancient texts.

"The New Testament Gateway: *Gospel of Thomas*" (*http://www.ntgateway. com/noncanonical-texts/gospel-of-thomas/*). Like everything else on Mark Goodacre's outstanding Web site, this page includes links to the very best material on the Web dealing with the *Gospel of Thomas*.

"*Gospel of Thomas*: Bibliography, Coptic and Greek Texts" (*http://www. agraphos.com/thomas/*). This site contains reconstructions of the Coptic text from NHC II and the Greek fragments from P. Oxy 1, 654, 655.

INDEX

Other Books in the Series